FLYTYING
for Beginners

To Oscar

You made me see the stars
and hear the music.
Live, love, learn, and enjoy life always.

Grandad

FLYTYING
for Beginners

Learn All the Basic Tying Skills
via 12 Popular International Fly Patterns

BARRY ORD CLARKE

THE FEATHER BENDER
EST. 1961

Skyhorse Publishing

Skyhorse Publishing books may be purchased in bulk at special discounts for sales promotion, corporate gifts, fund-raising, or educational purposes. Special editions can also be created to specifications. For details, contact the Special Sales Department, Skyhorse Publishing, 307 West 36th Street, 11th Floor, New York, NY 10018 or info@skyhorsepublishing.com.

Skyhorse® and Skyhorse Publishing® are registered trademarks of Skyhorse Publishing, Inc.®, a Delaware corporation.

Visit our website at www.skyhorsepublishing.com.

10 9 8 7 6 5 4 3 2 1

Library of Congress Cataloging-in-Publication Data is available on file.

Cover design by Merlin Unwin
Cover photo credit: Barry Ord Clarke

Print ISBN: 978-1-5107-7046-1
Ebook ISBN: 978-1-5107-7171-0

Printed in China

Contents

Glossary of Flytying Terms

Abdomen
Rear section of the fly body behind the thorax.

Barb / Fiber
A single fiber of hackle, or a strand of hair. Also, the sharp projection between the point and bend of a hook which prevents it slipping out of the fish's mouth.

Bead head
A metal, plastic or glass bead that is threaded onto the hook shank behind the eye of the hook. They add weight and an attractor element. Sometimes slotted or counter sunk.

Butt
A turn or two of material to separate the abdomen from the tail of a fly.

Cape
Bird skin from the neck/back area which is covered in hackle feathers.

CDC
The feather from a duck's preen gland. Prized in flytying for its natural buoyancy.

Collar hackle
Traditional style of hackle that is wrapped around the hook shank behind the head of the fly.

Counter wrap
Technique in which a rib of tying thread, tinsel, or wire is wrapped around the hook shank in the *opposite* direction to the body material. Used to reinforce fragile material like peacock herl.

Dry fly
A fly which is designed and dressed in such a way that it sits on the surface of the water. To a trout it appears as a fly sitting on the surface about to take off, or perhaps one falling onto it, exhausted and spent.

Dubbing loop
A loop of tying thread used to spin dubbing or other material into a dubbing noodle (a brush-like rope).

Dun
Dun is the stage of a mayfly's development between nymph and adult, a phase in the lifecycle which often prompts a trout feeding-frenzy. Dun is also a dull grayish-brown color of hackle.

Emerger
An aquatic insect about to hatch and fly off the water. Imitated by fly patterns which hang in the surface film (eg., the Klinkhamer).

Flare
To make a bunch of fibers, such as deer hair, fan out when compressed with tying thread. See step 18 page 101.

Floatant
Substance which the angler applies to dry flies to help them float longer. It comes in many forms: gel, liquid, and paste which all stop your dry fly absorbing water. In powder form it dries an already soaked fly.

Guard hairs
Long, stiff hairs which lie over the softer shorter under-fur on an animal's pelage (eg., beavers, hares, foxes, etc.).

Hackle
Feather from the neck (or sometimes saddle) of a rooster. Flytyers wrap hackle feathers around the hook in various styles adding buoyancy to dry flies.

Hair wing
The type of wing popular for modern dry flies. Most commonly made from deer hair, elk hair, or calf tail.

Herl
The barb of a feather, normally from a peacock or ostrich, used for dressing the abdomen, thorax, and wing cases on many fly patterns.

Nymph
The immature form of some invertebrates, particularly aquatic insects, which undergo a gradual metamorphosis before reaching the adult stage. Fished sub-surface.

Rib
Open spiral turns of wire or tinsel over an underbody of another material.

Parachute Post
An upright vertical wing that can be made of either synthetic or natural material to create the support around which is wrapped a horizontal parachute hackle.

Parachute hackle
A hackle wrapped horizontally around a parachute post.

Palmered hackling
The technique where the hackle is wrapped in an even open spiral along the whole body of the fly.

Saddle
Part of a bird skin from the rump area, which is covered in the long, slender feathers used as hackles for dry flies.

Segmentation
The creation of contrasting divisions along the abdomen of a fly, to imitate the natural banding pattern of an insect's body.

Streamer
Style of fly that imitates a bait fish. Usually tied on a long-shank hook (streamer hook). Fished sub-surface.

Tail
The part of the fly that extends past the hook bend. On a dry fly the tail is often used to support the fly on the water's surface.

Tag
A short, brightly colored tail or the very rearmost material wrapped at the bend of the hook.

Thorax
The forward section of the fly body between the head and the abdomen.

Under fur
The fine, soft, dense hair that is located under the longer guard hairs on an animal's pelage. They lie close to the skin. Useful for dubbing but they need to be combed away when making deer hair wings.

Wet fly
A fly designed to be fished under the water, representing a nymph or very small fish.

Whip finishing
A simple slip-knot technique used for tying off the tying thread or finishing the head of a fly.

Wing case
The flat area that lies over the thorax of a nymph. This can be made of various natural and synthetic materials.

X-tie
This is an X-shaped wrapping technique used to hold a hackle 90° from the hook shank. Made by crossing the tying thread over the hackle stem and hook shank from left to right and then right to left.

Introduction

This is a guide book for those totally new to the art of tying flies. Until now, learning flytying from a book has not only been challenging, but often the cause of great frustration, with photographs or diagrams making even the elementary techniques difficult to grasp. Step-by-step images help a reasonably proficient flytyer understand the stages in making a fly, but for the new beginner, there will always be a gap between each step-by-step image, which can be bewildering! Seeing the manual maneuvers that take place in these blank spaces can make the difference between success and failure for a new beginner.

For this reason, I aim to take learning flytying to a whole new level via this book. I want to make the essential techniques and skills required easier to master than ever before.

The techniques you will learn in this book are the building blocks on which all successful fishing flies, even the most complex ones, are based. Follow my recommendations for tools and materials, pay special attention to fly proportions, and first watch the videos of me demonstrating the relevant techniques before you start to tie each fly. Then with a little patience and a good deal of practice, you will soon be tying beautiful flies.

Each technique and pattern in this beginners' book has a five-stage tutorial.

- Guidance and instruction on all tools, materials, and techniques used for each pattern.

- The very best step-by-step images to illustrate every single stage in great detail, from inserting the hook in the vise to the finished fly.

- Explanatory text for each step-by-step image that leads you through each technique and pattern.

- Unique among beginners' books, each pattern is supported by a Quick Response (QR) code, which instantly links you to my YouTube channel and the accompanying video for each fly pattern. Here you can watch me tie that pattern. Video is an ideal medium to see any special procedure or technique at first-hand, before you start to tie using the book.

- You can also send me your questions in the comments box of each instructional video, if you are struggling, need advice, or just have a query!

If you follow the instructions carefully, and use the book correctly, along with its online support, you can master techniques, proportions, uniformity, and perfection in your flytying.

Materials List
for tying all the flies in this book

Hooks
Standard Dry: # 12, 14, 16
Long Shank Nymph: # 10, 12
Standard Emerger: # 10, 12
Standard Streamer: # 6, 10

Materials
Tying threads: black, grey, red, brown, tan, and olive
Lead wire (fine)
Hare's mask
Gold oval tinsel #14
Ring neck pheasant tail
Varnish
Copper wires: gold, silver, and black
    flat copper wire
    round copper wire (medium)
Peacock eye feather
Deer hair (undyed)
Super Fine dubbing: olive, black, gray, and blue dun
Gold Holo braid

Tape eyes: small, yellow
Squirrel "zonker" strips
Brass beads: large
Silver beads: small
Marabou: olive
Krystal Flash: pearl
Chenille: olive, black, fluorescent green
Peacock dubbing: olive
Para-post wing: white
CDC feathers: natural
Elk hair: bleached
Polypropylene yarn: black
Mallard flank feathers
UV resin

Hackles
Cock hackles: olive, black, grizzle dyed brown, golden badger, blue dun

How to Use This Book

The fly patterns I will demonstrate in this tutorial have been listed by their degree of learning difficulty, and in each one you will learn different techniques. I have carefully chosen each of the twelve patterns to demonstrate the tying techniques you need to learn in order to become a competent flytyer. At the start of each pattern, I indicate which of my accompanying background beginners' techniques videos I recommend you to watch. Together the twelve patterns cover the most common insects and food items on the trout's menu: midges, caddis flies, mayflies, ants, and bait fish. They are also twelve of the very best international fishing patterns to represent these food items, so you will know how to tie flies that catch fish in most trout-fishing situations.

The index at the end of the book tells you where to find particular patterns, techniques, materials, or tools. Each of the twelve patterns is listed with a dressing (i.e., all the tying materials you will need, with recommended hook style and size). These are listed in the order that I use them in the book's step-by-step images and in the twelve videos. This will help you to select and prepare your materials for each pattern beforehand. I recommend you follow the tying sequences in the book in the order they appear because they are the building blocks for your skills.

Tools. Here I cover the essential flytying tools used in this book. I explain their purpose and applications, and this section also serves beginners as a reference when you use one of the tools in a new pattern. I have also made videos of some of the key tools (linked in the book via QR code) so you see them in use.

Materials. Here I explain each material used in some depth so that you learn what to look for when buying them. Quality, color, sizes, variants: this chapter provides you with essential knowledge to understand each material, its qualities, uses, and applications.

I recommend that you start by downloading the free QR code app for your mobile or tablet for scanning the QR codes—or using the other links provided—to watch the videos of me demonstrating the relevant techniques for that fly and then of me tying the specific pattern. Then return to the book and follow the step-by-step instructions, to tie at your own speed and leisure, referring back to the video if need be.

Once you are confident about the first pattern, and have tied at least half a dozen that you are satisfied with, move on to the next pattern and continue thus, until all twelve patterns and their techniques are mastered.

Anatomy of the Fly

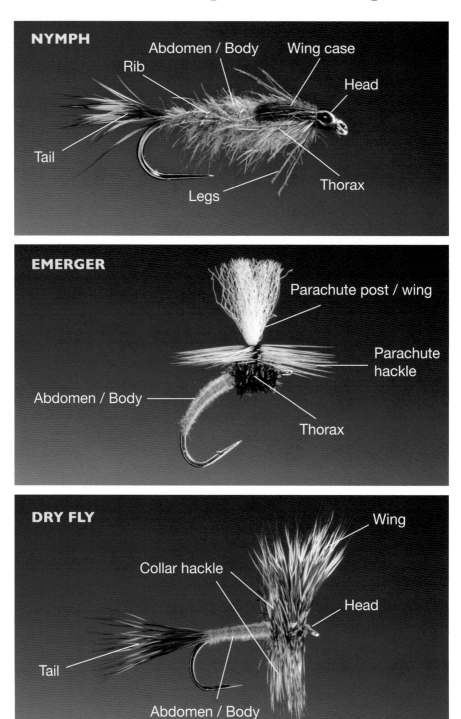

NYMPH

Abdomen / Body

Rib

Wing case

Head

Tail

Legs

Thorax

EMERGER

Parachute post / wing

Parachute hackle

Abdomen / Body

Thorax

DRY FLY

Wing

Collar hackle

Head

Tail

Abdomen / Body

Flytying Materials for the Beginner

For the complete beginner to flytying, the sheer amount of materials available, both natural and synthetic, can be, to say the least… perplexing! Not to mention hooks which come in different models, sizes, finishes, and makes…

The materials listed in the next few pages, like the twelve fly patterns you will tie with them, have been carefully selected for their individual qualities and their suitability for the techniques we are going to learn. And you will go on to use them as your expertise in tying flies grows, for these materials are used internationally in thousands of other fly patterns.

Getting to understand the materials you are going to use as a flytyer will increase your chances of tying good flies and will make your tying experience more enjoyable. More importantly, you will gain an appreciation of their potential, applications, and limitations.

Once you start tying, you will quickly learn how much easier it is to tie with quality materials. When buying your materials, try to visit a shop with a decent flytying department with a wide selection of materials, and staff who are themselves flytyers to help you choose and answer your questions.

Even in these shops, the materials will vary. Always be aware that, no matter how similar they look, no two natural materials are the same. Feathers and fur come from individual birds and animals, whose lifestyles, geography, diet, and time of year they were culled are all contributing factors to the quality of the material. A common mistake when buying materials, not only for beginners, is to take the first packet hanging on the peg in a shop. If you are going to buy a brown cock/rooster cape, depending on the quality, these can range from a few dollars to several hundred dollars per cape! Like any purchase, you look for value for money. Let's say for instance that there are eight brown capes hanging on the wall of the shop: look through all the packets and choose the one that works best for the patterns you wish to tie. You will spot varying quality in hackle size, color, markings, sheen… not to mention quantity. This rule should be applied when purchasing all natural materials, which at first glance all look the same, but only under closer scrutiny are the defining qualities noticeable.

Synthetics, on the other hand, are identical from packet to packet, but you may find the naming of some synthetics a little confusing, because the same or similar materials may appear under different marketing names.

Anatomy of the Hook

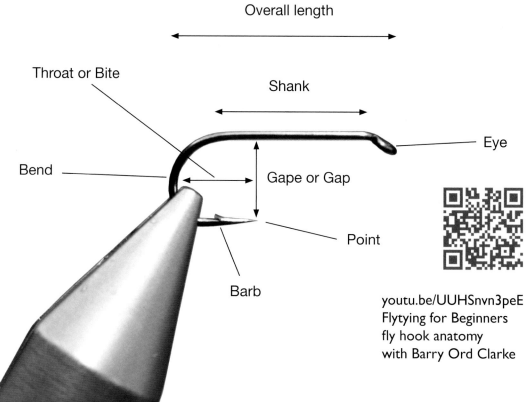

Overall length

Throat or Bite

Shank

Bend

Gape or Gap

Eye

Point

Barb

youtu.be/UUHSnvn3peE
Flytying for Beginners
fly hook anatomy
with Barry Ord Clarke

HOOKS

A hook's size, shape, and weight reflects the insect or animal body size and shape it is going to imitate; and how it will sit on the water surface or swim in it!

Dry fly hooks

Dry flies float on the surface of the water, so dry fly hooks are normally fine diameter, made from standard (S) or fine or even extra fine (XF) wire so that there is minimum weight in the hook, making the fly float better.

Wet fly and Nymph hooks

Wet fly (top right) and nymph hooks (bottom right) are both normally made with a heavier diameter wire (XH = extra heavy) to give the hook extra weight, in order to make it sink. Nymph hooks are normally longer than wet fly hooks (2XL or 3XL) to imitate the long, slender bodies of many naturals.

Emerger and Grub hooks

These hooks normally have more bend than the straight hook shank (C = curved). Emerger hooks (top right) are designed to imitate hatching insects that are hanging in the surface film of water. The curved hooks help the flytyer to imitate this stage, with the rear part of the body of the insect submerged and the thorax and wing case above the surface. One of the most successful emerger flies is the Klinkhamer. Grub hooks (bottom right) have no straight shaft and are totally curved.

Streamer hooks

Because almost all streamer patterns are tied to imitate bait fish, the hooks used for streamers tend to reflect the natural body shape of a small fish in various sizes. Most streamer hooks are made of standard (S) or heavy diameter wire (XH = extra heavy) and come in various shank lengths (3XL, 4XL).

Hook size

Hook sizes cause confusion for most flytyers, let alone beginners. The number on a hook generally refers to its size in relation to other hooks in the series, but there is no industry standard and different manufactures have different standards for applying numbers to their own sizes.

The most important thing to remember is that the size number on a hook packet is a "relative size" not an actual measurement of a hook. The higher the number, the smaller the hook size with #28 a very small hook. The lower the number, the larger the hook size with #1 a very large hook.

CDC

CDC is an abbreviation for Cul de Canard, which roughly translates as the end of the duck. These CDC feathers grow around the gland that produces preening oil. This highly water-repellent oil is used by birds to dress their feathers, and is at its most water-repellent on ducks, which would drown without the oil. The preen oil makes these feathers float extremely well and is thus ideal for tying dry flies. The tiny barbules on the CDC feathers also catch air bubbles which makes them effective on dry fly and emerger patterns. Besides its excellent floating properties, CDC is great for casting because as soon as the cast ends, the hackles reopen and bounce back perfectly into shape. CDC is available in natural and many dyed colors (but I much prefer it undyed).

CHENILLE

Chenille (French for caterpillar) encompasses various yarns which radiate short fibers at right angles to their axis. Modern chenille-type yarn has been created electrostatically by "flocking" fine synthetic fibers onto a single strand core pre-coated with a tough adhesive. This is sold as Suede chenille, Ultra chenille, or Vernille. Various diameters of chenille are available, from micro to jumbo and all colors imaginable. Chenille is mostly used for the bodies of nymphs and streamers.

DEER HAIR

Deer hair is widely used by international flytyers, as it is versatile and readily available. Deer hair is often wrongly described as "hollow" but it is not hollow like a drinking straw: rather, each hair is filled with a honeycomb of tiny cellular air pockets. Deer hair from a winter coat has a much larger diameter hair which gives your flies an exceptionally springy feel and invaluable buoyancy. Deer hair sold in tackle shops comes from a wide range of species, including seventeen subspecies of deer, elk, and moose, each with their own characteristics and uses. Good deer hair feels thick and spongy when squeezed, with a noticeably more fatty/waxy feel to the touch. When buying deer hair, look for hair that is straight, has even tips and good markings in the shade or color you require. It comes in small and jumbo patches in various natural, bleached and dyed colors. Deer hair texture falls into three categories, all with different degrees of compression and flaring when it comes to flytying.

Fine Dry fly. Not noted for flaring. Excellent for down wing patterns, traditional dry fly tails and wings and also parachute posts.

Medium General purpose hair. Flares to around 45 degrees or more, excellent for Caddis and Comparadun patterns, extended bodies, smaller spun, and clipped patterns.

Coarse Spinning hair. Flares up to 90 degrees and is used for larger clipped bodied patterns for hair bugs and predator patterns. This hair is available in the largest range of dyed colors.

HACKLES

Next to your vise, this is the most expensive material investment, and it's worth spending money on. Hackle traditionally arouses the greatest passion amongst fly tyers. Cock / rooster capes of particularly good quality or rare color and those with sufficiently short barb length to enable small dry flies to be tied—these have always been highly prized.

Many traditional colors have recently reappeared in qualities that far exceed anything that was obtainable in the past. These developments come at a price, however, and the tyer will have to pay for top quality cock cape or saddle from the best known American "genetic" hackle farms.

The dry fly cape is a tyer's most prized possession. I have seen friends become ecstatic over obtaining that special cape or saddle in that unique color. There is a whole load of mystique that surrounds the hackle, without doubt the most used material in flytying. It has so many applications: tails, dry fly and streamer wings, quill bodies, feelers, palmered, parachute, paraloop, and traditional hackles just to name a few.

An appreciation of quality hackle comes only with practice and viewing and handling many kinds and grades of hackle over time. Some of the most important points to look for are:

Color This is usually the first consideration. The best capes have an even and uniform color that conforms to one of the traditional color designations. It is worth noting, however, that even when a cape lacks uniformity of color or is of a "nondescript" color, it may still be of excellent quality in all other respects. Such capes are often less expensive and can be used as they are, or used for dyeing.

Condition The healthiest and strongest birds produce the best conditioned feathers. Dr Tom Whiting, owner of Whiting Farms, has said that when choosing birds for breeding he considers not only color and quality but also the character of the birds. No matter how good a color a bird may appear to have, a poor spirited bird will not get a good deal in the pecking order, so its health and condition—and therefore feather quality—are unlikely to be the best. Such a bird rarely produces top quality hackle.

The appearance of a cape is often a good first indicator of general condition if not ultimately of quality. Birds in good health and condition seem to "glow" and the individual feathers are clean and springy. Poor condition often manifests itself as a tatty pecked appearance with thin patches possibly indicating poor diet, infestation, or disease.

Feather count It is clearly desirable for a cape to have as many feathers of a useful size as possible. Some indication of feather density can be gained just from feeling between finger and thumb the thickness (depth) of a cape, where it starts to broaden at the shoulder. Bending the cape at this point will make the feathers fan and stand proud from the skin and separate. Individual hackles can then be examined and assessment made of the numbers, size and distribution.

The best quality capes have high numbers of hackles with barbs short enough to tie the tiniest dry flies. These capes command the highest prices. So if you are tying larger fly patterns, it's pointless buying expensive hackles suitable for tiny hook sizes 22–28. Indeed, if your tying mainly involves sizes 10–16, then a lower grade cape will not only be cheaper but will probably have more hackles in the larger sizes you will need.

Usable hackle length Look closely at the characteristics of individual hackles. The best cock hackles display the highest barb count along the shaft (stem) and they provide the longest portion of "usable hackle." This portion is called the "sweet spot" and is where ideally all the barbs on each side of the shaft are of a uniform length. The hackle shaft, the 'backbone' of the hackle, should be fairly thin and flexible to allow easy bending for wrapping around the hook shank. Hackle shafts that are too thin can break and those that are thick have little flexibility and are bulky when tied in. Hackle stems that are brittle—possibly through bird age or poor drying technique—are almost useless.

The best hackles have a long sweet spot and high barb density along the shaft, allowing more barbs to be wound onto the hook with the minimum turns of hackle. The longest sweet spots to be found are on some of the top grades of saddle hackle. These hackles are so long that many flies can be tied from a single hackle.

KRYSTAL FLASH

Krystal flash is very fine twisted Mylar strands with tiny reflective surfaces along its length. A few strands added to a wing create a spectacular sparkly effect which shines through the winging material as pin-prick sparks of light, resembling the flash scales of a bait fish. Available in every color and color combination imaginable, in both pearlescent and metallic finishes.

DUBBING

Dubbing is made from the natural furs and hairs of various animals and synthetic fibers, with many popular dubbings being a blend of both. The chosen dubbing material is then spun onto or into your tying thread, to form a "noodle" of dubbing which is then wrapped around the hook shank to form a body or thorax.

Originally, natural dubbing such as beaver and musk rat fur were used for dry fly bodies as they have natural water-repellant oils which help the fly float better and longer. Other furs like rabbit and fox were used for nymphs as these absorbed water and helped the fly sink. Today modern synthetics with a huge range of colors textures, translucency and reflective surfaces are available. Many tyers blend their own particular mix of shade and style of dubbing, using the advantages of both natural and synthetic materials.

HARE'S MASK

This refers to the mask and ears of the European brown hare. Individual masks range in natural colors from pale tan to various shades of brown and almost black. The texture and length of hair varies from different parts of the mask: everything from a fine soft underfur, to varying lengths and textures of stiff guard hairs. The hare's ears are covered with short stiffer hairs, almost completely without underfur. A mixture of hair from the ears and the mask makes a dubbing which is used in hundreds of fly patterns.

Here's a tutorial on how to prepare your own hare's ear dubbing

> youtu.be/Mxb7lGeElCs
> Hare's ear dubbing prep part I

Here's a tutorial on how to mix and blend the hare's ear dubbing:

> youtu.be/tTnpalhG7Gk
> Hare's ear dubbing prep part 2

MALLARD FLANK FEATHERS

These are the naturally-barred gray flank feathers from the side of a mallard drake. They are generally sold in three sizes: small, medium, and large. Dyed, they are a good substitute for the more difficult-to-obtain wood duck flank. They can be used for a multitude of techniques and tasks from tails to wings on both dry flies and streamers. When purchasing, try to avoid packs of mixed unsorted hackles as you will find that much of the material is unusable. Choose packs that are sorted by size; or purchase a whole mallard skin.

MARABOU

These fluffy plumes originally came from the African marabou stork. These birds have been strictly protected for many years and today the substitute comes from the thighs of the domestic turkey. Turkey marabou is a favorite material for winging lures, streamers, and saltwater patterns. The individual fibers are very soft and mobile, producing a sinuous, lively action underwater. Marabou is also used extensively in imitative patterns such as dragon and damselfly nymphs, leeches, and worms. Available in every color.

PARA-POST WING

Para-Post is a water-resistant yarn which lends itself extremely well for the wings and the posts of parachute patterns on dry flies, and as trailing shucks on emergers. This is available in many colors.

BEADS

Beads for flytying come in many forms and sizes. They are available in brass, steel, tungsten, plastic, and glass—in just about any color! Beads are primarily mounted just behind the eye of the hook or under the thorax. They add additional weight, a little extra bling, a hot spot (a trout trigger), or a combination of all three.

Buy the correct bead size for the hook you are using. It's not always easy to get the bead past the hook barb or around the bend when threading them on, so getting the right size for the hook is vital.

There are several different types. The two most common are:

Slotted: These have one small hole a little larger than the diameter of the hook wire on one side and a open slot on the other side. Recommended for beginners as they fit most hooks.

Counter sunk: These have one small hole on one side and one larger countersunk hole on the other. These are limited to which hooks they can be used on. Less expensive than slotted beads.

PEACOCK HERL

The eye tail feather from the peacock (male) provides us with this famous flytying material called herl. Covered in short iridescent green fibers, it is used for wound bodies, thoraxes, butts, heads, and wing cases in hundreds of fly patterns. For stripped herl patterns the best herl to use is from just under the eye of the tail feather. The herls are stronger here than others found on the tail.

PHEASANT TAIL

The least expensive and most common pheasant tail used in fly tying is from the Ring Neck pheasant. The best feathers come from the center of the tail of the male bird (cock pheasant). These long center tail feathers have the longest fibers and normally the best chevron barred markings. These have many applications as tails, bodies, wing cases, and legs, just to name a few. No two tail feathers are alike, so when buying pheasant tails, look at them all in the shop and choose the ones with the longest fibers and most vivid colors and markings.

POLYPROPYLENE YARN

A smooth-textured synthetic yarn available in many colors. Less dense than water, polypropylene yarn is particularly suited to dry flytying, such as wings, parachute posts, shuck cases, wing cases. Silicon-coated polypropylene yarn is even more water repellant than standard polypropylene.

SQUIRREL ZONKER STRIPS

There are 267 squirrel species around the world and all could be used for flytying! However the most commonly used are: gray squirrel, red squirrel, pine squirrel, and fox squirrel. Although the tails are used for hairwing, salmon, and seatrout patterns, the body fur makes outstanding zonker strips and dubbing. Pine and gray squirrels have a beautiful salt and pepper color mix that can be dyed and blended as dubbing to further extend their usefulness to the flytyer.

TYING THREAD

There are so many tying threads available today and they all have different properties. The flytyer will learn to choose the one best suited to the task at hand in terms of thickness (denier) stretchability, waxed or un-waxed, the material it's made from, and last but not least color. Tying thread is something the flytyer gets to understand and they will compile a collection of over time. All the flies in this book are tied with Gordon Griffiths, Sheer 14/0, a lightly waxed, fine, but very strong tying thread which is available in many colors.

UV RESIN

There is a multitude of UV resins available to the flytyer, some better than others. UV resin is a light-cured acrylic which is activated with the help of a UV torch. The greatest advantage of UV resin is that, unlike epoxy, there is no waiting time for drying. Excellent for coating bodies, heads, and wing cases of all manner of patterns. It is available in various viscosities and colors: a great addition to any tying kit.

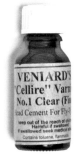

VARNISH / HEAD CEMENT

The varnish in flytying is primarily used for finishing the head of the fly. This gives the tying thread a protective coat and stops the fly from unravelling. For this purpose I recommend a fine "thin" clear varnish that will be soaked into and under the tying thread, resulting in a solid, super-hard finish that will prolong the life of the fly. If you like a smooth glass-like finish to the heads of your flies, several coats are recommended after the previous one has dried.

WIRES & TINSELS

Again, these are available in so many differing gauges, colors, weights, and materials, all of which suit different styles and jobs for many patterns. Used mostly for bodies, tags, and ribs of every type of fly, wires and tinsels are one of the least expensive materials that the flytyer uses, and in different sizes, forms, and colors they are normally accumulated en masse over the years.

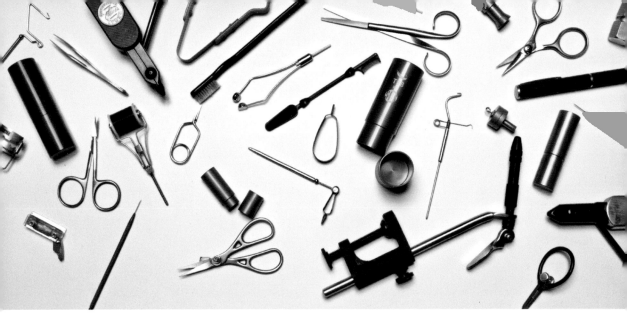

Essential Flytying Tools

If you are reading this book, it is possible you have already acquired a flytying kit. When you open your kit for the very first time, the first thing you notice is the overpowering smell of moth balls. This is used to keep feather and fur-eating insects at bay, and to stop them making a smorgasbord of your materials. Having got over the aroma, you'll see that the newly purchased kit is filled with what looks like, at first glance, a fantastic array of shiny tools and materials from the most exotic foul and beast.

Unfortunately, these kits differ dramatically in content, quality, and usefulness. A poor kit is probably also one of the main reasons for failure among new beginners. Learning to tie flies with inferior tools and materials is an uphill battle.

If you haven't acquired a kit and have access to a reliable flyfishing store with a good flytying department and knowledgeable staff, ask if they can help put a basic kit together to your budget, with quality tools and materials tailored to the patterns that you wish to tie. When it comes to tools and materials, you generally get what you pay for. On page 8, I have listed all the **materials** you'll need to tie all the flies in this book.

Although other flytyers may disagree with this choice, here is my personal recommendation, for the **essential tools** that will help you master the necessary techniques and skills to tie not only fishable, but also handsome flies!

VISE

This is the single most expensive item you need as a flytyer, so your choice should be made carefully. You should consider how many and what type of flies you will tie, and what size hooks you will be using. Beyond the prime function of holding the hook securely, modern vises incorporate a number of additional functions of varying usefulness. Adjustable height, jaw angle, and full rotation are standard in most good models.

Vises are available in many different designs and price bands. The best way to buy a vise that suits not only your budget but also tying style and requirements is to visit a retail store with a good selection of designs and price range. Ask the staff to point out the advantages and disadvantages of the different models and makes and try them out for yourself.

SCISSORS

It's unreasonable to expect one pair of scissors to do all the cutting jobs required when tying flies. Eventually you will need at least two: one high quality pair with sharp, short, fine points, for all the delicate work with tying thread and natural materials; and a second, less expensive pair for heavier work such as cutting tinsels, wire, etc. If you intend to tie many deer hair flies, it is also useful to have another pair with serrated blades. These grip the deer hair and enable flush cutting.

When buying scissors, make sure that your finger and thumb fit comfortably in the handles, so you can slip out of them easily and exchange them for other tools without the need for a second hand.

HACKLE PLIERS

It's much easier to position each turn of a delicate hackle on the hook precisely with the use of a hackle plier. They come in many designs and price ranges. I use and recommend a rotary model. The rotary model will keep the hackle from twisting when wound. It's important that whichever model you choose, the sprung jaws have a secure grip, even on the finest hackle points.

A good tip for all models, which improves their gripping quality without damaging the materials to be held, is to glue two small pieces of superfine sandpaper on the gripping side of each jaw, then trim them down to fit the edges of the jaws. This will stop materials slipping out of the jaws when maximum tension is applied.

youtu.be/nFHfAkiOvXU
Flytying for Beginners
improving your
hackle pliers with
Barry Ord Clarke

BOBBIN HOLDER

This is the tool that holds and dispenses your tying thread. A poor quality bobbin holder can be infuriating. It is really worth investing in a good quality ceramic bobbin holder, which is far superior to other models. The ceramic tubes are more durable than even the highest quality surgical steel, which eventually becomes worn and develops grooves that start to fray and cut the tying thread.

The wire arms of a bobbin holder need to be adjusted to accommodate the particular size of spool being used and to set the desired tension. The tension should be light enough for you to easily draw off thread, while still being tight enough to hang under its own weight without unwinding. Setting the tension on a bobbin holder is as follows: For **less tension**, pull the two wire arms outwards from each other, and to **increase tension**, the opposite. Beginners should experiment with their bobbin holder and learn to fine-tune the tension.

DUBBING NEEDLE

This is probably the most simple tool for flytying, but it's one of the most useful. Dubbing needles have many tasks to perform: applying varnish to finished flies, picking out dubbing, splitting hackle fibers, mixing resins, etc. The dubbing needle (as opposed to the handle) should be short (4–5cm), fine, and sharp. Avoid long dubbing needles—they are impossible for precise work. Your workspace when flytying can quickly become chaotic, and it's easy to spend more time looking for your dubbing needle than tying flies. Therefore I have several dubbing needles of mixed diameter standing upright in a piece of foam. The tip of the dubbing needle quickly becomes covered with a build-up of varnish, epoxy and head cement. This can be scraped away with a blade, but I keep my needles clean with another method. I have a 35mm film canister that I have filled with wire wool. All I need to do is push my built-up dubbing needle through the canister top down into the wire wool a few times and the needle is as new!

DUBBING SPINNER

Resembling a small spinning top, this is a very useful tool indeed. Once you have made a dubbing loop with tying thread, this tool keeps the loop open so that your dubbing material can be placed in-between the two lengths of tying thread. You then simply spin the dubbing spinner and it traps and twists the material in the loop into a tight rope. This rope, or noodle, forms the body of the fly.

youtu.be/_rB3pOEJFhc
Flytying for Beginners using a dubbing spinner with Barry Ord Clarke

HAIR STACKERS

When a bunch of hair, whether deer, squirrel, or badger, is cut from a patch of hide, the fiber tips are always uneven. When tying the tails and wings of many fly patterns, all the hair tips should align with each other, creating a neat square tail or wing. This simple but extremely effective tool simplifies this task. Once you have cut the required amount of hair, remove all the soft underfur and shorter hairs from the bunch. Now place the hair bunch, tips first, into the two-part stacker and rap it firmly on a hard surface four or five times. This will drive the hair tips down to the same level at the base of the stacker. Carefully turn the stacker horizontal, remove the base and all the hair tips are exposed—level and ready for use.

youtu.be/lxKdTzfdiPY
Flytying for Beginners using hair stackers with Barry Ord Clarke

HAIR COMB/BRUSH

This is an essential and inexpensive tool if you intend tying with deer hair. For nearly forty years I have used, perfectly happily I may add, an old worn-out tooth brush for this job. You use a little comb for cleaning hair before stacking and spinning. The brush can also be used for teasing out fibers in dubbing for a more bushy effect.

UV LIGHT TORCH

This is a torch for curing UV resin. When buying a UV light torch, make sure that it is in the correct frequency range for your chosen resin, otherwise you may find that the curing time increases. Replace the batteries in your torch on a regular basis. If your curing takes longer than it should, and the finish on the resin remains a little tacky, the batteries are on their way out!

WHIP FINISHING TOOL

This is a tool for tying off the thread with which you have tied your fly. This task is probably the one that has caused more frustration for flytyers than any other! A perfectly sufficient finishing knot (half hitch) can be tied with your fingers. But with a whip finisher you can position each turn of the tying thread precisely when making the end knot, resulting in a perfect head.

This is almost impossible to learn from a book, so watch the video!

youtu.be/RLaKGGapua4
Flytying for Beginners using a whip finisher with Barry Ord Clarke

Basic Flytying Techniques

Here are the essential techniques which 99 percent of all fly patterns require. Although basic, they have to be learned, practiced, and mastered. They will make your tying experience more enjoyable, and also result in quicker and better flies.

I demonstrate all of these techniques within the twelve step-by-step patterns featured within this book. Each of these background techniques which you will need to master in order to tie a particular fly are also listed at the beginning of each relevant fly chapter.

I. SECURING THE HOOK IN THE VISE

Firstly, make sure that your vise is anchored firmly to the table or pedestal, at the correct height for you to work comfortably. There should be no involuntary movement in your vise. A vise that moves when used is hopeless to tie on.

Select the correct hook style and size for the pattern to be tied. Place the hook bend in the open jaws of the vise and adjust the jaw tension, so it gently holds the hook in position. Now taking hold of the hook eye, pivot the hook until the hook shank is horizontal. Once the hook is correctly positioned, tighten the cam lever or screw.

2. ATTACHING THE TYING THREAD

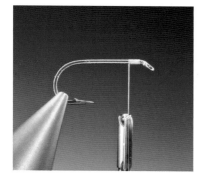

You start every fly by attaching the tying thread, not with a knot, but by running the thread in even, touching turns, trapping the initial turn with the second turn and repeating these steps. Attaching the tying thread and winding it down the shank like this also provides a non-slip bed which acts as a firm base for the rest of the tying.

Many flytying instructions don't even mention *attaching* the thread (although it's an essential first step!) they simply open with: "Run the thread down to a point above the hook barb, in close touching turns."

QR CODE FOR VIDEO LINK: see Thread Control QR code (opposite)

3. BOBBIN TENSION

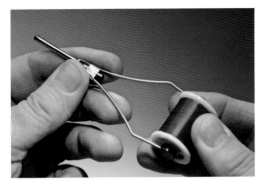

Over the past twenty-seven years I have held hundreds of flytying courses and demos. In just about every single course, I have met frustrated students who have been tying with the bobbin tension so tight that they are bending the hook or breaking the tying thread every few wraps! Or, at the other end of the scale, the tension is so slack that when they release the bobbin from their hand, it unspools and falls to the table or the floor!

What you need to achieve is a tension that has a little resistance when you pull on the bobbin. If further tension is required, let's say when spinning deer hair, this can be applied by using the palm of your hand as a brake on the spool.

youtu.be/EwVo8uu3PEg
Flytying for Beginners setting bobbin tension
with Barry Ord Clarke

4. THREAD CONTROL

Thread control is one of the most overlooked aspects of flytying, but when mastered, you will use it in every single fly that you tie.

Beginners are often a little heavy handed when they start tying, and find that breaking off the tying thread comes more naturally than just about anything else. Try attaching your thread to the hook and slowly and gradually applying more tension with your bobbin until the thread breaks. Make a mental note of the breaking strain and apply it to your tying!

How to quickly change your thread from a round profile to a flat profile with just a twist of your bobbin is a skill that applies to just about every single technique there is. This, plus how to split your thread to make a dubbing loop, and how to control your thread when tying in materials are all demonstrated in the thread control video. Watch, learn, and practice.

youtu.be/0HmdSDxXC5I
Flytying for Beginners attaching thread
& thread control with Barry Ord Clarke

5. DUBBING TECHNIQUES

Synthetic dubbing

Natural dubbing

This is a method for applying loose fibers—natural, synthetic, or a mixture of both—to your tying thread. These fibers are then wound onto the hook to form a body or thorax. The most common mistake is to try to apply too much dubbing—less is more. There are many different techniques for doing this. I have included the most common techniques for both synthetic and natural materials in the videos.

youtu.be/rGlwgBoCVDk
Flytying for Beginners three simple dubbing techniques with Barry Ord Clarke

youtu.be/wOkZQJGtcWY
Flytying for Beginners dubbing techniques with fur & hair with Barry Ord Clarke

6. COLLAR AND PARACHUTE HACKLES

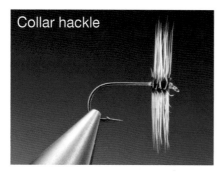

Collar hackle

Parachute hackle

Here you will learn two techniques for hackling a dry fly. Using a good quality hackle is the key to success here. Modern genetic hackle capes and saddles bred specifically for flytying are expensive but they can be purchased in small, carefully-selected packs of a few hackles, in different sizes and colors. This book also teaches the **palmered hackle** within the tying sequence for the Elk Hair Caddis (pages 97–102)

youtu.be/tllwhx9a8ZQ
Tying a traditional dry fly hackle with Barry Ord Clarke

youtu.be/jukEKgwNZyk
Tying the parachute perfect hackle with Barry Ord Clarke

7. HOW TO TIE WINGS

There are many different and useful techniques that can be learned for creating wings for dry flies, but here in the book we will address four of the most important ones: CDC wing (p37), feather wing (p59), elk hair wing (p97 and pictured left), and split hair wing (p113).

8. WHIP FINISHING

Making a couple of half hitch knots just behind the hook eye is the best way to finish a fly. This can be done using just your fingers or with a whip finish tool. I recommend using a whip finish tool, especially if you have large, rough hands. Whip finishing is almost impossible to learn from a book, so I suggest that you watch the video, as many times as necessary and practice!

youtu.be/RLaKGGapua4
Flytying for Beginners using a whip finisher with Barry Ord Clarke

9. VARNISHING THE HEAD

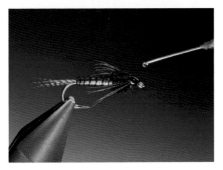

Applying a coat or two of varnish or head cement further strengthens the whip finish knots and stops the fly from unravelling. Nowadays many tyers strive for the perfect head with a smooth, glossy, almost mirror-like finish, but this is mostly for the sake of aesthetics.

For precision varnishing I recommend that you use a short dubbing needle, just 4–5cm long, as anything longer is difficult to use.

Place your left hand on top of your vise with your thumb straight out horizontally. While holding your dubbing needle, use your thumb to support your right hand when varnishing.

Apply only a tiny drop of varnish at one time: this will reduce the chances of spillage. You can always apply more, but never less! A single application of clear fine varnish to the head will be sufficient for most fishing flies.

How to Tie the
Zebra Midge

The midges are one of the most abundant insect groups found in fresh water ecosystems, and therefore one of the most important to the fly fisherman. There are literally thousands of different species of biting and non-biting midges in various stages of life cycle, which are available to trout throughout the whole year and which represent a significant amount of the trout's diet in both still and running water.

One of the most popular artificial flies in recent years is the Zebra midge. This little pattern ticks every box for a great fishing fly. It's inexpensive, it doesn't require any special materials or techniques, it's quick and simple to tie, and last but not least, it catches fish.

Midge larva come in a wide range of sizes and colors including blood red, olive, grey, brown, and black. So all you have to do is change your hook size and the color of your tying thread and you have most subsurface situations covered with this one simple pattern.

You can also tie it with or without the bead head. Without the bead head, the fly will fish higher in the water and be more effective when midges are hatching; and with the bead head it will fish deeper as a midge larva.

Inexpensive brass beads are available in many colors and sizes and are good enough for the bead head on this pattern, but they won't sink as fast as the more pricey tungsten beads. When buying beads, make sure that you purchase the correct size and that they will thread easily on to the hook size and shape that you are using. Best to get advice from your tackle dealer and buy the hooks and beads together for this, as there is no industry standard in sizes.

Although the thorax is only a few wraps of peacock herl, make sure that the herl you choose is thick with fibers. The best herl for this is taken from just below the "eye" on the peacock tail feather. The herls located here have the best volume and are also the most robust.

WHAT YOU'LL LEARN

- How to secure a slotted bead head
- Simple wire ribbing
- Building a peacock herl thorax
- Best way to varnish a bead head

TYING TIPS

- Tie some with and some without the bead head
- Make each turn of wire rib evenly spaced
- Varnishing a bead head

WATCH THE VIDEO

youtu.be/ertfUO608q0

Flytying for Beginners Zebra Midge with Barry Ord Clarke

Background technique videos 1–4, 8, 9 (see pages 26–29)

THE DRESSING

Hook: Small grub hook size 12–20
Thread: Black
Head: Small slotted tungsten bead
Body: Black tying thread
Rib: Silver wire
Thorax: Peacock herl

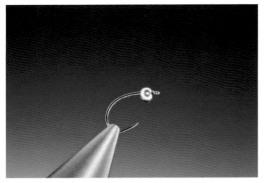

1 Slide a small tungsten bead onto the hook shank. Secure the grub hook in the vise as shown.

2 Load your bobbin holder with black tying thread. For these small flies it's better to use a tying thread of a small denier, 14/0 tying thread is perfect for this.

3 Attach your tying thread directly behind the bead head and then lean your thread into the bead's slot. Make several wraps, turning the bead as you go, until a build-up of thread stops the bead rotating. This will hold the bead firmly in position. Now run your tying thread a little way down the hook shank in tight turns.

4 You will now need to cut a 10cm length of bright silver wire.

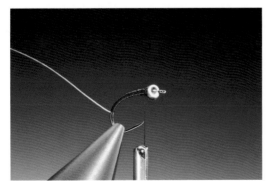

5 Lie the wire along the hook shank to the back of the bead head and wrap your tying thread back over it, to behind the bead head. Secure the end of the wire with a few more turns of tying thread.

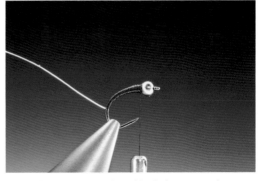

6 Run your tying thread back down over the wire to the hook bend and back up again. Now spin your bobbin counterclockwise so your thread gets a flat profile. Wrap your tying thread several times to form a tapered body as shown.

continued next page

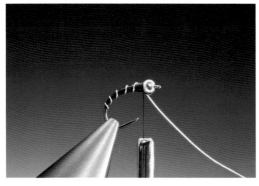

7 You can now make five or six evenly spaced turns (clockwise) of silver wire, up towards the bead head. Secure the wire with a couple of wraps of tying thread.

8 While retaining tension on your bobbin twist the wire until it breaks clean off.

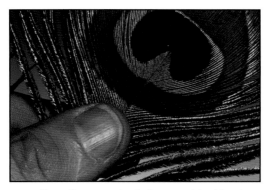

9 You will now need a single peacock herl for the thorax. The best herl for the job comes from just under the eye of a peacock tail feather.

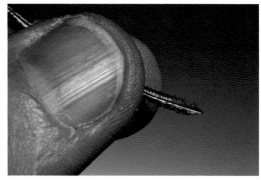

10 Once you have selected a herl, trim 2–3cm off the butt end.

11 Tie the peacock herl in by the butt end a little behind the bead head with the herl fibers pointing backwards.

12 Attach a hackle plier to the end of the peacock herl and make a few wraps forward until you reach the bead head. Secure the herl with a couple of turns of tying thread.

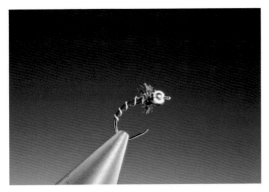

13 Remove the excess peacock herl and give it a couple of whip finishes close to the bead. Remove your tying thread.

14 To varnish the head, turn the hook vertically in the vise as shown. Now using your dubbing needle, apply a single drop of varnish to the hook eye. You should see the varnish disappear under the bead. This will give a solid finish to the bead head; repeat this until no more varnish is sucked in under the bead head.

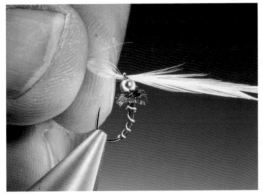

15 When you first start tying flies, varnishing heads can prove a little tricky, and it's easy to accidentally clog the hook eye with varnish. Here's a neat little tip that you can use on all flies. Take an unwanted hackle stem and pass this through the eye of the hook to clean out any surplus varnish.

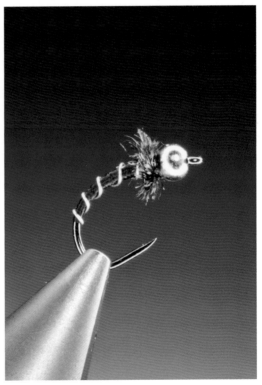

16 The finished Zebra Midge.

continued next page

How to Tie the
F-Fly

Although there are many variants of this pattern, I stick to the original. All that is required is tying thread and a couple of natural CDC hackles.

There is, however, a little technique to mastering this pattern. A lightweight, fine denier tying thread works best. I recommend Sheer 14/0 which is a lightly waxed, super fine but strong thread that you can spin clockwise so that it attains a round profile, or spin it counterclockwise for a flat profile. Perfect for making fine flat bodies with little volume. It's also very reasonably priced and comes in all the most important colors.

The body should be fine and slender with a slightly decreasing taper towards the rear of the fly. Less is more! When it comes to the wing, I suggest that you invest in the very best quality CDC you can afford. This is the same with all natural materials: I can't emphasise how important top quality materials are for improving your flytying and thus your results! You can get away with buying bulk packs of CDC, which are probably the most reasonably priced, but you will find that much of the CDC in the pack is too small or only useful as dubbing. However there are also companies which sell small packs of carefully selected CDC feathers which only contain enough for making a dozen or so flies—but the quality is generally excellent. Again, materials are something that you will learn to understand and appreciate the more you tie.

The F-fly was designed by the famous Slovenian fishermen Marjan Fratnik, back in the time when CDC was almost un-heard of. It can be used to great effect on stillwaters, fished static, or with gentle twitches. But where it really shines is on clear, slow-to-medium-fast running waters for grayling and trout. Fished in small sizes, on a long, delicate leader, it's also the perfect choice for shy and selective fish.

Don't be fooled by this simple little pattern: it's one of the few flies that I would just not go trout fishing without.

WHAT YOU'LL LEARN

- How to handle and tie CDC feathers to make simple, buoyant wings

- How to create a smooth, tapered body from your standard tying thread

- Mastering thread control

TYING TIPS

- Use a fine denier tying thread for this delicate pattern

- Select CDC with good even tips

- Use natural CDC colors (dyed ones can lose some of their floating qualities)

WATCH THE VIDEO

youtu.be/zusbn891Gdk
Flytying for Beginners F-Fly
with Barry Ord Clarke

THE DRESSING

Hook: Standard dry fly hook, sizes 14–18
Thread: Gray or beige
Wings: 2 or 3 natural CDC hackles

Background technique videos 1–4, 7, 8, 9 (see pages 26–29)

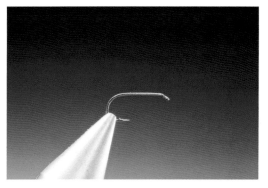

1 Secure your dry fly hook in the vise with the hook shank horizontal.

2 Load your bobbin holder with tan or beige tying thread.

3 Attach your tying thread a little way back from the hook eye and cover the whole hook shank with a fine foundation of tying thread.

4 Run your tying thread back to the start position. Now spin your bobbin gently, counterclockwise. This will give your tying thread a flat profile.

5 Once your thread has attained a flat profile start building a slender body using neat touching turns of tying thread.

6 When you have achieved the correct cigar-shaped body, end up with your tying thread a little behind the hook eye.

continued next page

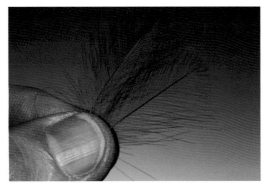

 7 Now select two similar-sized CDC feathers with plenty of fibers.

8 Place one CDC feather on top of the other, making sure that the tips are aligned as close as possible.

9 Pinching both hackles in your right hand, measure the wing, a little longer than the hook shank.

10 Switch hands, so you are holding the wing in your left hand and secure it onto the hook with a few turns of tying thread with your right hand.

11

Carefully trim away the excess CDC over the hook eye.

12 Now, starting behind the hook eye, build a small head with tying thread as you work your way back towards the wing. Tie it off with a couple of whip finishes.

13 Snip off your tying thread and give the head a tiny drop of varnish. Take care not to get varnish on the CDC wing.

14 If necessary, trim the rear of the wing down to an even length. It should be approximately the same length as the hook shank. See photo on next page for a darker feather variant.

continued next page

How to Tie the
Pheasant Tail Nymph

The original pheasant tail nymph was created by legendary English flytyer and fishermen Frank Sawyer around 1930. He designed the pheasant tail nymph to imitate the small mayfly nymphs on the southern English river Avon, where he was river keeper. Sawyer's original pattern used only pheasant tail fibers and fine copper wire instead of normal tying thread, to give the pattern extra weight. The modern variants of the PTN with which we are familiar, including the one illustrated here, bear little resemblance to Sawyer's original.

With only three materials plus tying thread needed for this pattern, it is nevertheless best to choose the right materials. At first glance, one pheasant tail feather looks like any other pheasant tail feather. But take a good look at a few cock pheasant centre tail feathers side by side, and you will see they are very different! Not only does the background color and shading on each tail differ immensely but the black chevrons vary from light to dark and thin to thick. But probably the most important factor is the fiber length. Normally the best marked feathers with the longest fiber length are found centre top of the cock ringneck pheasant tail.

The pheasant tail nymph has all the characteristics, shape, form, and proportions for a generic nymph. In other words, you can apply the exact same tying technique used here to imitate many other nymphs found on the trout's menu—just change the colors, materials, and size.

If you wish to add extra weight to this pattern you can do so using a few wraps of lead wire under the position of the thorax. You should do this at the very beginning, at Step 1 of the following sequence.

Another extremely popular variant of the pheasant tail nymph is with the addition of a gold bead head, either at the head of the fly (as per the Zebra Midge, see page 33) or tied in at the thorax, under the wing case. The bead head not only adds additional weight but also a bit of bling!

TYING TIPS

- Always make sure you keep the pheasant tail fibers parallel when wrapping around the hook shank

- Use a bright copper wire for the rib

- Aim for symmetry and correct proportion between the tail, legs, and wing case to create a more natural-looking nymph

WATCH THE VIDEO

youtu.be/AypIHLATNjY
Flytying for Beginners
Pheasant Tail Nymph with
Barry Ord Clarke

Background technique videos 1–4, 8, 9 (pages 26–29)

THE DRESSING

Hook: Long shank nymph hook size 8–16
Thread: Brown
Tail: Cock pheasant tail fibers
Abdomen: Cock pheasant tail fibers
Rib: Fine or medium copper wire
Legs: Cock pheasant tail fibers
Thorax: Peacock herl
Wing case: Cock pheasant tail fibers

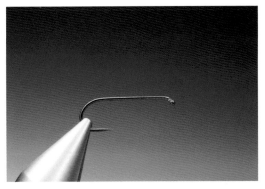

1 Secure an extra-long nymph hook in the vise, so that the hook shank is horizontal.

2 Load your bobbin holder with brown tying thread.

3 Attach your tying thread about a third of the way down the shank and wrap a foundation of thread over the central section of the hook shank, until the thread hangs vertically near to the hook point.

4 Firstly find a cock pheasant centre tail feather with strong markings and long fibers. To get all the points of the pheasant tail fibers even for the tail, take a small bunch between your finger and thumb and slowly pull them at 90° from the stem of the feather until all the points are level. Now, still holding the bunch tight so the points remain level, cut them away from the feather shaft with one swift scissor cut.

5 You now have a nice bunch of pheasant tail fibers for the tail.

6 Tie in the tail fibers on top of the hook shank. The tail (off to the left here) should be approximately half of the hook shank length.

PHEASANT TAIL NYMPH

continued next page

7 Now you will need a 10cm length of copper wire.

8 Tie in the copper wire fairly close to the head and wind the tying thread along the length of the hook shank. Leave the remainder of the pheasant tail out over the hook eye; we will need these for the wing case.

9 Repeat steps 4 & 5 and cut another bunch of long pheasant tail fibers. Tie this new bunch in as shown, by the tips, along the top of the hook shank, tight into the tail base.

10 Before you start wrapping the pheasant tail fibers to form the abdomen, make sure that the fibers are not twisted. Holding the whole bunch, wrap the fibers (clockwise) forward over the abdomen, and tie off with a few wraps of tying thread in the same position as the previous bunch.

11 Trim away the excess pheasant tail, as shown.

12 Take hold of the copper wire and make 4–5 evenly spaced turns (counterclockwise) over the peacock herl abdomen. If you would like a little extra weight to the nymph, make a few more close wraps of wire by the thorax. Secure the wire with a few turns of tying thread.

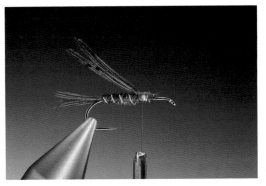

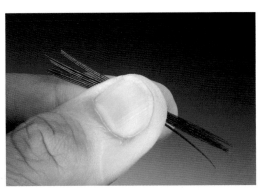

13 Cut away the surplus copper wire. Now fold all the pheasant tail fibers back over the copper wire and tie down, taking care to keep them all on top of the hook shank.

14 Once again cut a smaller bunch with pheasant tail fibers with the tips level. This bunch will be the legs and the wing case of the nymph.

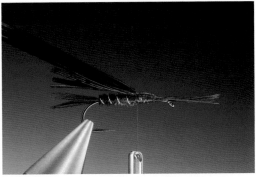

15 Place the tips out over the hook eye, approximately the same length as the tail. Tie down the bunch on top of the copper wire as shown.

16 Select two peacock herls with nice bushy fibers.

17 Tie in the peacock herls, butt ends first, and cover the ends with tying thread, finishing just behind the hook eye.

18 Now take the peacock herls and wrap them over the whole thorax making sure they don't twist and cross each other. Tie off behind the hook eye.

continued next page

19 Trim off the excess herl. Divide the pheasant tail tips into two equal bunches and fold them back and along each side of the thorax to form the nymph's legs. While holding these in place, secure them in position with a few wraps of tying thread.

20 The legs should look like this from the side view.

21 Now take the bunch of pheasant tail fibers you have collected for the wing case, and fold them over the thorax, again taking care to make sure that all the fibers are parallel and don't cross over each other. Secure with a few turns of tying thread.

22 Once secure, your tying thread should be a little back from the hook eye, as shown here.

23

Carefully trim off the excess pheasant tail fibers at an angle over the nymph head. Care should be taken not to cut your tying thread by accident here!

24 Now with wraps of tying thread, build up a small neat head. Complete with a couple of whip finishes and snip off the tying thread.

25 You can now give the head a couple of coats of varnish.

26 The finished Pheasant Tail Nymph as seen from above. Note the proportions and symmetry in the tail, body, wing case, and legs.

continued next page

How to Tie the
Hare's Ear Nymph

The gold-ribbed hare's ear nymph, as it is often called, is found in many variants, from the ultra simple to the ultra realistic. The one illustrated here is my variant, which falls somewhere in-between both. The one thing that they all have in common is a body of hare's ear dubbing that is ribbed with a gold tinsel.

Hare's ear dubbing is something that every flytyer should learn to make and use, as it's one of the elementary but essential techniques. Alongside peacock herl and pheasant tail, hare's ear dubbing is regarded as one of those wondrous materials for fashioning a buggy insect body for which trout seem to have a fatal fascination!

Although called "hare's ear dubbing" this is actually a mixture of coarse and soft hair from the hare's ears and mask. When assembling the hair for this dubbing, the key is to select a good mixture of hair shades, textures and lengths, the scruffier the better! These can then be blended by rubbing them together in the palm of your hand, until the desired shade and texture is achieved.

For this style of hare's ear dubbing I use a dubbing loop made from tying thread. With your tying thread hanging at the tail base, pull on your bobbin holder so that you have about 20cm of tying thread out of the tip of your bobbin holder. Now place the index finger of your left hand on the tying thread and fold over the thread so as to form a loop, and secure it to the hook with a couple of turns at the tail base. Make sure that where the two thread ends meet at the tail base, they are close together. Keeping the loop open with the index finger of your left hand, load the loop with hare's ear dubbing and insert your dubbing spinner. You can now remove your finger and spin the loop to make the dubbing brush.

The gold tinsel rib over the abdomen of the fly not only creates a little flash that emulates the small gas bubbles trapped on the body of an ascending natural, but when wrapped in the opposite direction to that of the dubbing (clockwise/anti-clockwise) it also doubles as a reinforcement, holding the hare's ear dubbing in place and protecting it from damage from trout teeth.

For the wing case and legs of the nymph, select an appropriate bunch of pheasant tail fibers. These should be long and have all the tips even, before tying in. The legs should be approximately half the hook shank length over the hook eye. Once you have attached the pheasant tail tips just behind the hook eye, wrap your tying thread back over the pheasant tail, towards the abdomen. Make sure that when you reach the abdomen, the pheasant tail fibers

are tied down so they are the same width as the abdomen. The wing case, when tied over the thorax, should go from broad to thin at the hook eye end (see step 22).

WHAT YOU'LL LEARN

- Making hare's ear dubbing

- Spinning a dubbing brush

- Counter-wrapping the body material and the rib

TYING TIPS

- Mix your hare's ear dubbing well

- Keep the body tight and slender

- Make it as scruffy as possible!

WATCH THE VIDEO

youtu.be/fi9BhaoO-mE

Flytying for Beginners Hare's Ear Nymph with Barry Ord Clarke

Background technique videos 1–4, 5, 8, 9 (pages 26–29)

THE DRESSING

Hook: Long shank nymph hook size 6–12
Thread: Brown
Weight (optional): Fine diameter lead wire 0.4mm (0.015")
Tail: Small bunch of long hare's mask guard hairs
Rib: Fine oval gold tinsel
Abdomen: Coarse & soft fur from hare's ears and mask blended together
Wing case: Pheasant tail fibers
Thorax: Coarse & soft fur from hare's ears and mask blended together
Legs: Pheasant tail fibers
Head: Brown

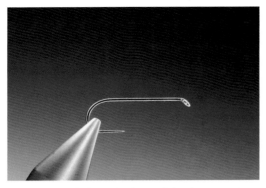

1 Secure the long-shank nymph hook in your vise as shown with the hook shank horizontal.

2 Load your bobbin holder with brown tying thread.

3 Now you will need a length of about 7cm of fine lead wire. Cut it with old scissors as this can blunt them.

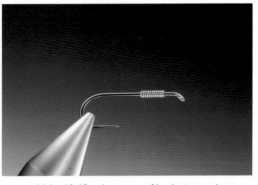

4 Make 10-15 tight wraps of lead wire as shown. This adds extra weight to the fly and makes it sink quicker, as well as adding a little volume to the thorax.

5 Attach your tying thread at the front of the lead wire as shown. This will act as a stopper and prevent the lead wire sliding forward.

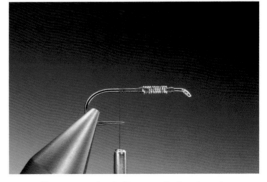

6 You now make 6–7 turns of tying thread rearwards over the lead wire and then at the rear of the lead wire make another few turns tight into the lead wire as a rear end stopper.

continued next page

7 Cut a little bunch of the long guard hairs from the hare's mask, Remove the softer shorter underfur from the bunch with your comb.

8 Keeping the tips roughly aligned, tie this bunch in, as shown. This forms the nymph's tail.

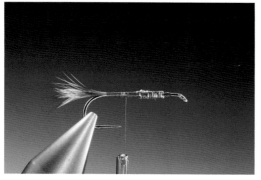

9 Once you are happy with the tail, secure the whole bunch with wraps of tying thread.

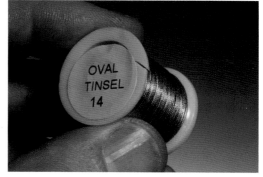

10 You will now need a short length (about 10cm) of oval gold tinsel for the rib.

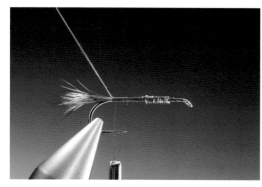

11 Place one end of the tinsel along the top of the hook shank and tie this in along the whole length of the abdomen finishing at the tail base as shown.

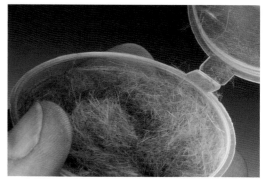

12 Now you will need your hare's ear dubbing.

FLYTYING FOR BEGINNERS

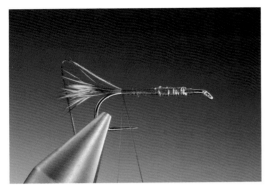

13 Make a dubbing loop (see pages 51–55 and page 28 dubbing techniques videos) with your tying thread at the tail base.

14 Fill the top two-thirds of the loop with a little dubbing mixture, insert your dubbing spinner, and spin the loop to make a spiky dubbing brush.

15 Wrap the dubbing brush (anti-clockwise) in tight even turns around the tail base and forward towards the thorax, taking care to cover the whole abdomen with dubbing. Secure the dubbing brush with a few turns of tying thread.

16 Take hold of the tinsel and make four or five evenly spaced turns (clockwise) forward and secure the tinsel over the lead wire. Cut away the excess tinsel.

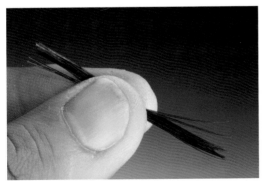

17 Now select a bunch of pheasant tail fibers, taking care that you have the tips level.

18 This bunch will be the legs and the wing case of the nymph. Placing the tips out over the hook eye, tie down the bunch on top of the lead wire as shown.

continued next page

19 Now make another dubbing loop at the thorax with slightly longer hare's ear dubbing and spin another dubbing brush a little shorter than the previous one.

20 Wrap the dubbing brush round the thorax and finish with your tying thread a little behind the hook eye. Cut away the excess dubbing loop.

21 Separate the pheasant tail leg fibers into two even bunches. These should be tied down on either side of the hook shank with a few wraps of tying thread.

22 Keeping all the pheasant tail fibers parallel, fold them over the thorax to form the nymph's wing case. While holding them in position, secure with a few turns of tying thread.

23

You can now carefully trim away the surplus pheasant tail fibers. Take care here not to cut your tying thread by mistake!

24 Starting tight behind the hook eye, make a few wraps of tying thread back over the cut pheasant tail ends and form a small neat head. Make one or two whip finishes and remove your tying thread.

25 Give the head a couple of coats of varnish, taking care not to get varnish on the thorax or wing case.

26 The finished Hare's Ear Nymph from the side, ready for use. On next page: a Hare's Ear Nymph viewed from above.

continued next page

How to Tie the
FLYING ANT

This flying ant is what we call a semi-realistic pattern with wings, body, legs and head. You can get away with fishing with much easier-to-tie patterns, but with this one, you will learn several good techniques that you can put to good use when tying other patterns.

Ants are probably the most important terrestrial insect for the fly angler, no matter where you fish. They are extremely poor aviators. When they leave the nest in large numbers to increase their chances of establishing a new colony, they are placed at the mercy of the wind and end up where it takes them.

If they are unlucky enough to come to rest on water, especially in large numbers, the fish can go into a feeding frenzy. In extreme situations I have witnessed the trout taking just about any artificial fly that is presented to them! But at other times they can be so selective that they will only take the perfect pattern with the right silhouette, color, and size. Therefore it's important to have a good imitation to hand.

The natural ants that you are most likely to encounter when fishing will be black, but on occasion can be red, so here are two other variants of this pattern that may be worth you tying, depending on how prevalent ants are for your own fishing. Both are exactly the same pattern but with a slight change in color.

The first is tied all in red, including the wings.

The second is the one that I have increasing success with, and it has a red rear body and a black head, simply a mixture of both. This pattern will float well, especially if treated with a fly floatant. But if your ant sinks a little when fishing, don't worry too much, because the naturals swim as well as they fly, so the trout are used to seeing them underwater too.

The Super Fine dubbing range is an excellent choice for most general dry fly patterns that require a dubbed body. It's available in twenty-four relevant natural colors which represent most insect groups.

WHAT YOU'LL LEARN

- Split hackle-tip wings
- Tightly dubbed synthetic bodies
- Trimmed hackle for lower profile presentation

TYING TIPS

- Pay special attention to body-part proportions
- Apply only a little dubbing at a time: less is more
- Select the correct size hackle for the hook size being used
- Once you get this pattern right, tie up a few and try to get them looking identical

WATCH THE VIDEO

youtu.be/W2VdhHGmchY

Flytying for Beginners Flying Ant with Barry Ord Clarke

Background technique videos 1–4, 6, 7, 8, 9 (pages 26–29)

THE DRESSING

Hook: Standard dry fly hook size 12–16
Thread: Black
Body: Super Fine dubbing (black), polypropylene yarn (black)
Wings: Dun cock hackle tips
Hackle: Brown saddle hackle
Head: Super Fine dubbing (black), polypropylene yarn (black)

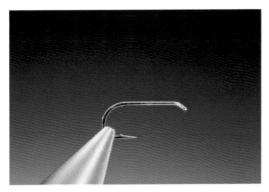

1 Secure your dry fly hook in the vise, as shown, with the hook shank horizontal.

2 Load your bobbin holder with the black tying thread.

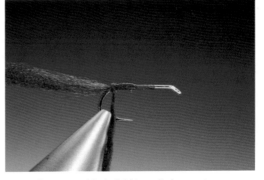

3 Attach your tying thread and wind it in touching turns to form a foundation over the center hook shank, until the thread hangs roughly vertically with the hook barb.

4 Cut a short length of black polypropylene yarn and tie this in at the rear of the hook.

5 You will now need a little black Super Fine dubbing.

6 Spin some black dubbing a little at a time onto your tying thread. Take your time and spin the dubbing nice and tight.

FLYING ANT

continued next page

7 Wrap the dubbing round the hook, starting a little down into the hook bend. Both the body and the head of the ant should be a very tight hard ball of dubbing.

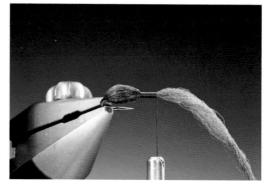

8 Once you are happy with the dubbed body, take hold of the polypropylene yarn and fold it back over the body and tie down as shown. Take care that the fibers in the yarn are parallel and tight.

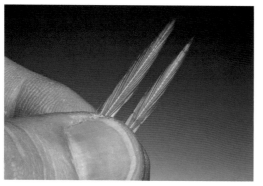

9 Select two small dun hackles of the same size for the wings.

10 Measure the wings to the correct length (roughly the same length as the hook shank) and then strip off all the fibers so the wings are at the end of a bare stem as shown.

11 Wrap your tying thread back to the abdomen, and tie in the first wing with a couple of turns of tying thread. You can now adjust the wing so it lies correctly, by pulling on the hackle stem.

12 Repeat Step 11 for the second wing. Take care that they are balanced and the correct length, one each side of the rear body. Once the wings are correct, trim off the surplus hackle stems, so they don't quite reach to the hook eye.

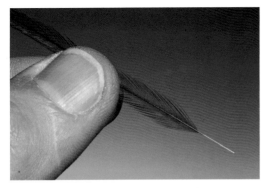

13 Prepare a brown cock hackle by stripping off the fibers each side at the base of the hackle stem.

14 Tie in your brown cock hackle by the stem with an X-tie (see Glossary page 6), so the hackle stands approximately 90 degrees from the hook shank.

15 You can now secure the bare stem of the hackle along the whole hook shank. If the hackle stem is longer than the hook eye, trim a little off before you tie it down.

16 Attach a hackle plier to your brown hackle tip and wrap the hackle in neat touching turns forward to your tying thread. Secure the hackle with a couple of turns of tying thread and cut away the surplus hackle.

17 Fold the polypropylene yarn back over the body and spin a tiny amount of black dubbing on your tying thread.

18 Wrap the dubbing, again nice and tight, to form the head of the ant. Take care not to crowd the hook eye—you should finish a couple of mm behind the hook eye.

continued next page

19 Now fold the polypropylene yarn nice and flat back over the head of the ant and secure with just a few wraps of tying thread.

20 Once the yarn is in position, trim away the surplus yarn and form a small neat head with tying thread. Make one or two whip finishes.

21 Remove your tying thread and give the whippings (where you've tied off the yarn) a little drop of varnish, taking care not to get any on the dubbed head.

22 We now have the finished flying ant.

23 If you would like your fly to fish deeper in the surface film of the water, you can carefully trim away the hackle fibers on the underside of the hook. This can on occasion give a better presentation for the trout.

24 A bird's eye view of the finished Flying Ant.

continued next page

How to Tie the
Montana Nymph

This was one of the very first nymphs I learned to tie many years ago as a new beginner. Having no internet or even step-by-step instructions, but with the help of a scalpel and a surgeon's precision, I meticulously dissected a Montana nymph artificial which I had bought, to learn the secret of its construction through de-construction. Not the easiest way to learn how to tie a pattern!

Although originally designed to imitate a large stonefly nymph which is native to North America, it has since become a modern classic which has brought fish to the net for fishermen all over the world, in both running and still waters, even where a stonefly nymph (the natural) has never been seen. This puts the Montana in the category of an attractor or searching pattern. No matter where you fish an attractor, the fish recognize it not as a specific insect, but as a general food item—and they go for it.

As with most nymphs, the Montana can be tied as a weighted or unweighted pattern, depending on how deep in the water column you would like the nymph to sink. The more weight, the quicker and deeper it will sink and fish.

When you are fishing bulky, weighted nymphs like the Montana, you want them to sink quickly. A good tip before your first cast is to give the fly a soaking in water and then give it a good squeeze. This will force out any small pockets of air that may be trapped under and in the chenille body, making the nymph sink immediately on hitting the water.

Over the years several other popular variants of the Montana nymph have also become standard patterns. One of the most common variants is the Green Montana, made by replacing the black chenille with olive chenille, and the green chenille with bright yellow chenille. The tail and hackle feathers remain black.

WATCH THE VIDEO

youtu.be/7CX2jgELul8

Flytying for Beginners Montana Nymph with Barry Ord Clarke

Background technique videos 1–4, 7, 8, 9 (pages 26–29)

THE DRESSING

Hook: Long shank nymph hook size 6–12
Thread: Black
Body: Fine diameter lead wire 0.4mm (0.015"). This extra weight is optional
Tail: Black cock hackle fibers
Abdomen: Black chenille
Wing case: Black chenille
Thorax: Yellow or green chenille
Legs: Black cock hackle
Head: Black thread

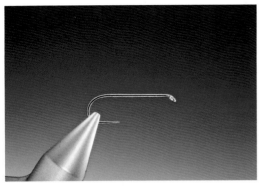

1 Secure your nymph hook in the vise as shown with the hook shaft horizontal.

2 Now you will need a short length (about 7cm) of fine lead wire.

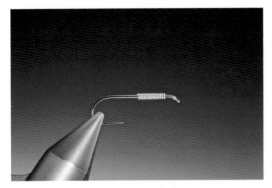

3 Make 10–15 tight wraps of lead wire as shown. This will not only add extra weight to the fly and make it sink quicker, but it will also add a little more volume to the thorax.

4 Load your bobbin holder with black tying thread.

5 Attach your tying thread at the front of the lead wire as shown. This will act as a stopper and prevent the lead wire sliding forward.

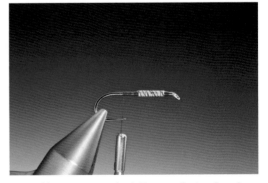

6 You can now make 6–7 turns of tying thread rearwards over the lead wire and then at the rear of the lead wire make another few turns tight into the lead wire as a rear end stopper.

continued next page

7 Select a large black cock hackle and strip away the downy fibers from the base as shown.

8 Cut a little bunch of the black hackle fibers, trying to keep the tips aligned. Tie this bunch in at the tail.

9 Now you will need some black suede chenille.

10 Cut a length (about 20cm long) and tie this in on top of the hook shank, between the tail base and the lead wire, no further, no less.

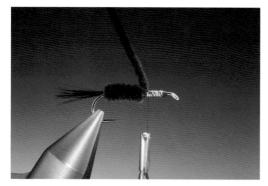

11 Now starting at the tail, carefully wrap the black chenille in tight even turns. Once you have reached the lead wire, secure the chenille on top of the hook shank with 3 or 4 tight turns of tying thread.

12 Take hold of the loose end of the chenille and fold it over so that the chenille forms a loop, and tie the loose end down as shown, on top of the lead wire. Make sure that you have no chenille over the hook eye.

FLYTYING FOR BEGINNERS

13 Now cut a short length (about 10cm) of fluorescent green chenille.

14 Hold the chenille in one hand, and using your thumb nail and finger, pull off the short fibers so you reveal the stripped core of the chenille as shown.

15 Using only the stripped core of the chenille, tie this down, once again on top of the lead wire. Take care that the green chenille starts tight against the black chenille loop.

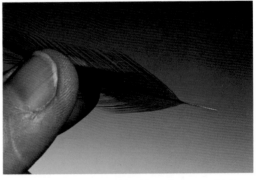

16 Select a black cock hackle and prepare this by stripping off the fibers at the base of the hackle. These will be the legs of the nymph.

17 Take hold of the hackle by its tip with your right hand and pull back the fibers at the tip with your left hand, so that you now are holding it as shown in your left hand.

18 While still holding the hackle in your left hand, tie it in, by its tip, tight into the black chenille loop and the green chenille. Wrap your tying thread forward so it's in position right behind the hook eye.

MONTANA NYMPH

continued next page

19 Take hold of the green chenille and make 4–5 tight turns forward, towards the hook eye. Take care not to crowd the hook eye! You must leave a little space here for finishing the fly. Tie off the green chenille with 3 or 4 turns of tying thread.

20 Carefully cut away the excess green chenille.

21 Attach a hackle plier to your black hackle and make 4–5 turns of hackle, take care that each turn of hackle sits neatly in-between each turn of green chenille as you wrap forward. Once you have wound the hackle to the hook eye, secure it with 3–4 turns of tying thread and trim away the excess hackle.

22 Take both strands of the black chenille loop and fold them evenly over the green chenille as shown. Tie them down behind the hook eye with a few turns of tying thread.

23

Carefully cut away the black chenille tight into the hook eye and secure the cut ends with a few more turns of tying thread.

24 Make a whip finish or two and snip off your tying thread. You can now give the head of the nymph a coat of varnish or two. Take care not to overdo it.

25 Bird's eye view of the finished Montana nymph. Notice how the black hackle-fiber legs angle slightly backwards.

26 Side view of the finished Montana Nymph.

continued next page

How to Tie the
Woolly Bugger

The Woolly Bugger is one of the iconic American trout flies. It doesn't represent any trout food item in particular. Instead, it suggests all manner of larger, sub-surface food for predatory fish.

When wet, marabou possesses a serpentine swimming action which cannot be matched by most other flytying materials. When this underwater action is combined with the jig effect of a heavy bead head, the Woolly Bugger swims and undulates tantalizingly with every retrieve. It has sealed the fate of many a fish.

It's getting the correct balance of marabou and weight that makes a good Woolly Bugger. If you make the marabou tail too long, it will wrap around the hook bend when you cast and it will fish ineffectively when retrieved. Use too much weight and the fly will not only drown rather than swim, but it will also prove difficult to cast.

Traditionally the Woolly Bugger was tied by its creator Russell Blessing with a black marabou tail, olive chenille body, and a black hackle. Although this is still a popular and killing combination, other colors such as all-olive, all-black, and some vivid combinations are also popular. With all the materials easily available in so many colors, the possibilities for effective variants are endless…

The palmered body hackle should be of the sort that has tapered fibers, long at the base of the hackle stem and progressively shorter towards the tip. This will give you a longer hackle at the head of the fly and a shorter one at the tail base. You should also look for webby hackles with thicker softer fibers, not the thin stiff hackle fibers required on a dry fly hackle.

Take care that each turn of hackle is pulled down in-between each turn of chenille on the body. This serves two purposes. It stops the hackle from slipping up and down the body when cast or fished; and when the hackle stem is down in-between the chenille, it protects the hackle stem from breaking when it comes into contact with the small sharp teeth of trout.

WHAT YOU'LL LEARN

- How to tie a marabou and Krystal Flash tail

- Palmered hackling over a chenille body, plus a dubbed collar

- How to fix in place a slotted bead head

TYING TIPS

- A shorter marabou tail avoids it catching in the hook bend when casting

- Step 4 is where you can add additional lead wire for extra weight—but don't overdo it!

- Use a drinking straw to smooth the hackles in the right direction

WATCH THE VIDEO

youtu.be/jwXruKxD0kw
Flytying for Beginners
Woolly Bugger
with Barry Ord Clarke

Background technique videos 1–4, 8, 9 (pages 26–29)

THE DRESSING

Hook: Long shank nymph or streamer hook size 4–12
Thread: Olive
Tail: Olive marabou & Krystal Flash
Rib: Copper wire
Body: Olive chenille
Hackle: Large olive cock hackle
Collar: Peacock dub (olive)
Head: Slotted bead head

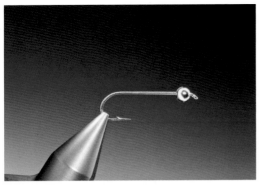

1 Slide the brass bead onto the hook shank. Secure the long shank hook in the vise as shown with the hook shaft horizontal.

2 Load your bobbin holder with olive tying thread.

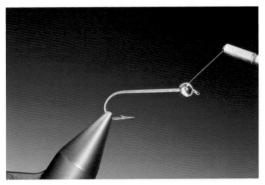

3 Attach your tying thread directly behind the bead head and make several wraps so as to hold the bead in position. Place the tying thread in the slot of the bead as shown and wrap until the bead stops turning. Run your tying thread a little way back down the hook shank in tight turns.

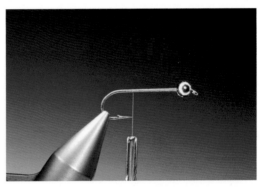

4 Now run the tying thread on down the hook shank until the bobbin is approximately vertical with the hook point.

5 Then select your marabou.

6 From the end of one of the marabou plumes, cut away the center tip.

continued next page

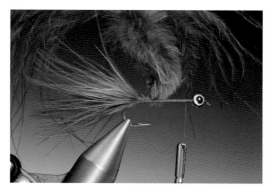

7 Now tie in the marabou on top of the hook shank, allowing the tip to protrude beyond the bend about the same length as the hook, or a little shorter if you prefer.

8 When you have secured the tail with a few more wraps of tying thread, lift the marabou and run your thread forward to behind the bead head.

9 Take hold of the marabou plume and twist the fibers together to form a "rope."

10 Lie the twisted marabou forward over the hook shank and secure a little behind the head with a few turns of tying thread.

11 Trim away the surplus marabou and tie down all the way back to the tail base.

12 You will now need some Krystal flash.

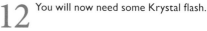

13 Select two or three strands of Krystal flash.

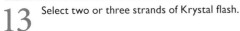

14 Tie these in at the tail base with one end out over the marabou tail and one end over the bead head.

15 Once you have secured these strands, take hold of the forward-facing Krystal flash and fold it back over the tail. Take care to evenly distribute the fibers around the tail for best effect. Secure with a few wraps of tying thread.

16 You will now need some copper wire.

17 Cut 20cm of copper wire and tie this in behind the bead then bind it along the whole length of the hook shank, finishing at the tail base.

18 Now take 15cm of olive chenille and tie this in at the tail base and along the whole hook shank, finishing with your tying thread behind the bead head.

19 Wrap the chenille in tight clockwise turns up the whole hook shank. Tie off the chenille a few mm behind the bead head and trim off any excess chenille.

20 Select an olive cock hackle similar to the one here and prepare by stripping off any downy fibers at the base of the stem.

continued next page

21 Tie in the hackle behind the bead head, so that it stands at approximately 90° from the hook shank.

22 Attach a hackle plier to the hackle tip and wrap your hackle backwards in a clockwise direction.

23 While holding the hackle in place with your hackle plier, take the copper wire and wind this in a clockwise direction catching the hackle tip and holding it down. Remove your hackle plier from the hackle and continue wrapping the copper wire in open even turns, up to the bead head. Secure the wire with a few tight turns of tying thread. Retain tension on your bobbin and twist the wire until it breaks clean off.

24 You will now need a little peacock dubbing.

25 Spin a small amount of peacock dubbing onto your tying thread.

26 Wrap the peacock dubbing rope between the hackle and the bead head as shown.

27 Once you have made a little peacock dubbing collar, make a couple of whip finishes behind the bead head and remove your tying thread.

28 Brush up the fibers of the peacock collar and trim off the Krystal flash fibers a little longer than the marabou tail. You can varnish the bead head as per instructions on the Zebra Midge (page 35).

29 This is optional but makes a better-looking fly. Wet the whole fly and stroke all the fibers and tail backwards.

30 Take a short section from a drinking straw, and cut a little notch in it as shown.

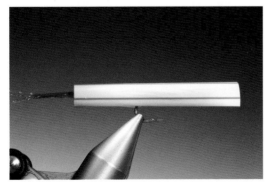

31 While the fly is still wet, place the straw over the head of the fly with the notch each side of the hook bend. Remove it from your vise and let the fly dry.

32 Once dry, remove the straw, to reveal the slightly more streamlined, finished Woolly Bugger.

WOOLLY BUGGER

continued next page

How to Tie the
Klinkhamer

Up in the top five questions from people when I am doing tying demos is: *Can you show me how to tie a Klinkhamer?* That, along with: *What's the correct way to tie a parachute hackle without a gallows tool?* So I normally tie the Klinkhamer to demonstrate both.

Preparation and material choice is important to achieve the correct body shape and hackle. Firstly, the correct hook should be used. This should have a curved shank, wide gape, slightly heavy wire and a straight eye.

The post on this fly has several functions. The Klinkhamer has an upright wing which, in combination with the slightly heavy wire hook, keeps the pattern on an even keel when fished. It's a sight indicator which helps immensely when locating the fly at a distance, in low light, or in rough water conditions and it's also the anchor point for our parachute hackle. The rear of the post, if trimmed correctly, will also be the foundation for our slender tapered dubbed body. When wrapping the base of the post, in preparation to accommodate the hackle, you want to make it nice and firm, so a drop of varnish or head cement will help with this.

A flytyer's challenge with most recipes for a parachute hackle is finishing it neatly. You always have to wind your tying thread forward through the thorax and hold the hackle fibres out of the way when you whip finish. The method I show here will avoid all that.

A few background tips here for the beginner. Prepare your saddle hackle by stripping off 10mm of the fibres from both sides of the hackle base (Step 13). Before you tie it on be sure to wrap your thread around the base of the post (Step 12) to form a stiff base on which to wrap the hackle. This will give you a much more firm and durable parachute hackle.

Repositioning the hook (Step 22) makes wrapping a parachute hackle as easy as wrapping a traditional collar hackle. Once done, hang your tying thread out of the way on your vice (Step 23).

Now you can wrap your hackle as you would a traditional dry fly collar hackle, taking care that each turn of hackle is close to the previous, all the way down to the thorax. When you reach the thorax, retrieve your tying thread from the vice and make one tight wrap over the hackle and one wrap under to secure it. Trim away the surplus hackle. Now trim your post to the required length, take your whip finish tool and make one whip finish, between the hackle and the thorax. Take care here not to trap any hackle fibres. Before you make the second and last whip finish, place a small drop of varnish on the tying thread close to the thorax. This varnish will be drawn into the whip finish as you tighten, and secure it.

The result should be a perfect parachute hackle.

WHAT YOU'LL LEARN

- How to create a parachute post and hackle

- How to shape a dubbed body

- Concealed para-post whip finish

TYING TIPS

- Be sure to trim the rear of the parachute post material to a fine taper

- Take care to trim the post to the correct length for the fly

- To avoid clogging the peacock herl thorax, apply varnish to the tying thread on the last whip finish

WATCH THE VIDEO

youtu.be/eNHShSju6xU

Flytying for Beginners
Klinkhamer with
Barry Ord Clarke

Background technique videos 1-4, 5, 6, 8, 9 (p28-30)

THE DRESSING

Hook: Standard emerger #6-14
Thread: Olive
Post: Para-post (white)
Body: Super Fine dubbing (olive)
Thorax: Peacock herl
Hackle: Golden (or silver) badger saddle

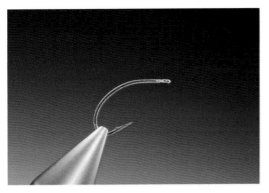

1 Secure your emerger hook in the vise, as shown, with the hook shank and eye horizontal.

2 Use a fine tying thread, preferably the same color as the dubbing for the body.

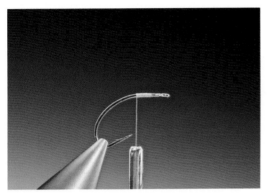

3 Attach your tying thread a little behind the hook eye and cover the first third of the hook shank with a foundation of tying thread.

4 Select the color of post material to be used. For most of my parachute patterns I favor white.

5 Cut a short length of post material. You may have to increase the thickness of your post material by doubling it or reduce the thickness of it by removing a few strands, depending on the hook size and your material of choice for the post.

6 Tie in the length, as shown, behind the hook eye, at the position where you will put the post. Make sure that you have enough para-post material at the rear for you to hold.

continued next page

7 Now lift the front of the material so it stands 90 degrees to the hook shank and make a few wraps of tying thread hard up to the front of the post to hold it in position.

8 While holding the rear para-post material in one hand, trim off the ends at a slight angle, so when covered with tying thread it will make a tapered body.

9 Now wrap tying thread over the rear post material and give the whole body a foundation of tying thread to form a slight taper. Take care not to overdo this: the body should be slim.

10 Spin some dubbing onto your tying thread and make a neat, tapered dubbing noodle. You can now wrap the noodle in tight touching turns over the body.

11 Continue with the dubbing until you reach the wing post and have made a neat tapered body as shown.

12 Now wrap your tying thread around the base of the wing post, first up and then back down to strengthen it. This will make wrapping the hackle much easier later on. Finish with your tying thread in front of the wing post.

13 Select a hackle of the correct size for your fly (see Fig. 28 for hackle proportion) and then strip off the fibers on both sides at the base of the hackle stem.

14 Tie in your hackle by the bare stripped stem end. Make sure the hackle is at 90 degrees to the hook shank.

15 Tie down the unwanted hackle stem on the underside of the thorax and snip off any excess. If you want to give the post an even better foundation on which to wind the hackle, place a tiny drop of varnish on the wrappings.

16 Wind your tying thread back to the rear of the thorax.

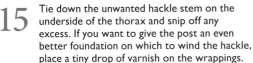

17 Now select a couple of strands of peacock herl.

18 Tie in the peacock herl tight into the dubbed body at the rear of the para-post. Return your tying thread to just behind the hook eye.

continued next page

19 Wrap the peacock herl forward in tight even turns to form the thorax. Tie off just behind the hook eye.

20 Trim away any remaining surplus herl. In order not to damage the herl, apply just a little varnish to the first cm of tying thread as shown.

21 Now make a whip finish or two, and snip off your tying thread.

22 Remove the hook from the vise and reposition it as shown. Now reattach your tying thread to the post's base and wind down close to the thorax.

23 Hang your tying thread to one side of your vise so as to keep it out of the way when wrapping the hackle.

24 Attach a hackle plier to your hackle tip and start wrapping the hackle round the base of the post all the way down to the thorax in neat touching turns.

25 Using a pair of tweezers, pull off a few fibers from each side of the hackle stem as shown. This will give you a clean finish when whip finishing. Then secure the hackle between the thorax and the last turn of hackle with a couple of turns of tying thread.

26 Snip off the surplus hackle, and trim down the para-post to the desired length.

27 Make a whip finish or two just below the hackle. Take care not to trap any of the hackle fibers. Just before you tighten your whip finish knot, place a drop of varnish on your tying thread again close to the thorax and then tighten. Remove your tying thread.

28 The finished Klinkhamer side view. The fly floats on the hackle with the body hanging underwater and the wing above the surface.

29 The Klinkhamer from above.

30 The Klinkhamer from below.

continued next page

How to Tie the
Zonker

The Zonker is an extremely easy to tie, semi-realistic imitation (i.e., a generic attractor pattern) representing most small bait fish.

Its originator in the 1970s was American fly tyer Dan Byford and it was quickly recognized the world over as a big fish fly. The original pattern incorporated a lead or tin sheet that was folded and glued over the hook shank and then cut to shape to make the underbody. My more contemporary body technique gives the Zonker a new life.

When this fly is viewed by a fish in reflected light, the shine and flashing of the UV resin-covered body braid, combined with the pulsating fur strip, makes it a first class bait fish attractor pattern. But when viewed by a fish in a back-lit situation (in silhouette) this pattern really comes to life, with the light penetrating through the transparent body and fur guard hairs.

The potential of the Zonker as a bait fish imitation pattern is limited only by your own imagination. There are any number of rabbit fur strip materials on the market in every color imaginable, not to mention Zonker strips made from fox, squirrel, mink, hare, etc. Along with the different colors of flat braid material available, the combination possibilities are endless.

The length of the strip shouldn't exceed twice the hook shank length: anything larger has a tendency to wrap around the hook shank when casting which spoils the swimming effect when fished.

Choose a clear UV resin with a medium viscosity so that you can manipulate the resin with a dubbing needle before you cure it. The resin should be applied only a little at a time and then cured at each step. This way, you can build up the body gradually and avoid mistakes. Once mastered, this technique will result in a perfect and identical minnow body every time. If you don't have a rotary vise you can detach your fixed vise from the bench and manually turn it to distribute the resin evenly on the fly body.

Eyes on a baitfish pattern are very important. They add an amount of realism and are regarded as an important predator trigger and attack point.

The Zonker, unlike bucktail and featherwing streamers, is an extremely robust pattern. If tied correctly, the dressing will normally outlive the hook. The hook should be a standard length streamer hook. If you are intending to fish in saltwater, use a saltwater-resistant hook.

- How to build a sparkling UV resin baitfish body

- Fur strip winging technique

- Application of baitfish eyes

TYING TIPS

- Apply the UV resin a little at a time and cure, before applying the next coat.

- It's worth spending time cutting the Zonker strip to the right shape before you tie it onto the hook

- If you don't have UV resin, you can tie this fly without it. Just add a little lead wire after Step 1 (see page 69 for guidance)

WATCH THE VIDEO

youtu.be/dwlH6Y0V6Xg

Flytying for Beginners
UV Zonker with
Barry Ord Clarke

Background technique videos 1–4, 8, 9 (pages 26–29)

THE DRESSING

Hook: Standard Streamer #6
Thread: Red
Underbody: Holographic flat braid
Overbody: UV resin
Wing/tail: Fur Zonker strip
Eyes: Tape eyes

1 Secure your hook in the vise, taking care that the hook shaft is horizontal.

2 Load your bobbin with red tying thread.

3 Attach your tying thread and run a foundation of thread along the hook shank until your tying thread hangs at the hook point, as shown.

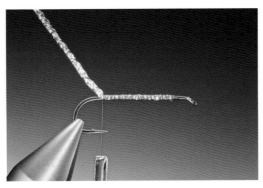

4 You will need some body braid in the color of your choice.

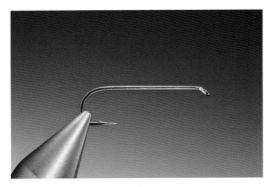

5 Cut approximately 20cm of holographic flat braid and tie this in along the top of the hook shank. Return the tying thread to the rear of the hook.

6 Now wrap the flat braid in close, even turns building a cigar-shaped underbody as shown. Tie off the braid at the rear of the hook (as shown) and cut away any excess. Finish with a rear whip finish.

continued next page

7 Take your UV resin and apply a very fine coat to the body. Take it slowly and apply only a little at a time. If you apply too much, don't cure it, remove some of the resin first.

8 Rotate your vise so that you centre the resin on the hook shank, and cure it with your UV torch.

9 Continue applying one thin coat of resin at a time and cure until the body size and shape as shown above is achieved.

10 Select two tape eyes, and stick one on each side of the head of the body. Once evenly in position, give them a fine coat of UV resin.

11 Cut a Zonker strip, about twice the length of the hook shank. Trim the tip of the strip to a taper, as shown.

12 Now moisten the fur at the end with a little saliva and make a parting of the hair on the strip as shown.

13 Place the strip on top of the hook shank and tie it down with several tight wraps of tying thread. Then make two whip finishes at the same position.

14 Once secure, remove your tying thread from the tail base and give the whippings a drop of varnish.

15 Now reattach your tying thread just behind the hook eye. Make another parting of the hair just above the tying thread.

16 With a couple of turns of tying thread, secure the Zonker strip in position. Then take hold of the strip and pull it tight along the UV resin body. Secure with a few tight turns of tying thread.

17 Now carefully cut away the excess Zonker strip skin which was protruding over the hook eye. Once done, form a neat head with a few more wraps of tying thread and apply a couple of whip finishes.

18 Remove your tying thread and give the head a fine coat of UV resin. The finished UV Zonker.

continued next page

How to Tie the
Elk Hair Caddis

This is probably the best known caddis pattern in existence, and rightly so. The EHC, as it is also known, is one of the best adult skating caddis patterns you can use. I myself have fished this pattern for over thirty years, and every season it provides me with great sport.

Most of the materials are readily available. The originator of the Elk Hair Caddis, Al Troth, recommends that you use bleached hock hair from a cow elk, which I have found almost impossible to obtain. But any quality bleached elk does a good job. Tan colored elk will also do a good job; it just makes the fly a little more difficult to see at a distance or on rough water, when fishing.

Deer hair is one of the materials not only beginners find challenging to work with, but so do many experienced tyers. Practice and good quality deer hair are the keys to success. When buying deer hair, like all natural materials, no two patches of hair are the same in terms of color, shade, hair length, hair density. You will need medium grade hair that flares to 45 degrees, unlike the more coarse, buoyant deer hair that will flare to 90 degrees. Look also for hair that is straight with fine, tapered unbroken tips. Beware that the tips haven't been burned away in the bleaching process. Quality hair will help you tie and will result in better flies.

This pattern has taken fish for me all over the globe, in all kinds of conditions, and not only during caddis hatches but also as a searching pattern, stripped with short fast pulls through the surface, when it's deadly!

I have had most success with this pattern in the smaller hook sizes from #14–16. When tying these smaller sizes, I prefer to use a finer hair. Although you can tie the elk hair caddis in various body colors, I have found that olive and orange are the most effective.

You can fish this pattern high and dry, so that it just floats on its hackle points, or you can fish it half drowned so that it gurgles like a popper when retrieved, and you can even fish it wet, just under the surface.

A brilliant all-round pattern.

WHAT YOU'LL LEARN

- How to tie a palmered body hackle—a really useful technique for creating bushy, buoyant flies
- Reinforced copper wire palmer rib
- How to create an elk/deer hair wing
- Cleaning and stacking deer hair

TYING TIPS

- Dub the body nice and tight
- Don't make too many hackle turns
- Clean the hair for the wing very thoroughly

WATCH THE VIDEO

youtu.be/A98qPGVtzBl

Flytying for Beginners Elk Hair Caddis with Barry Ord Clarke

Background technique videos 1–9 (pages 25–29)

THE DRESSING

Hook: Standard dry fly hook size 10–16
Rib: Extra fine copper wire
Thread: Tan
Body: Super Fine dubbing olive or color of your choice
Wings: Elk or other deer hair (bleached or tan)
Hackle: Brown cock hackle

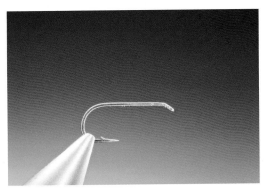

1 Secure your dry fly hook in the vise, as shown, with the hook shank horizontal.

2 Load your bobbin holder with tan tying thread.

3 You will need some fine copper wire for the rib.

4 Attach your tying thread and run a foundation over the entire hook shank. Cut a 20cm length of fine copper wire and tie in along the whole hook shank until the thread hangs roughly in line with the hook barb.

5 Select your chosen color of dubbing for the body. Take a small amount of dubbing and spin it onto your tying thread.

6 Now make a couple of clockwise wraps around the hook shank to anchor the dubbed thread. Then twist the dubbing around the thread again to make it tighter and wrap towards the head in touching turns to form a tight dubbed body.

continued next page

ELK HAIR CADDIS

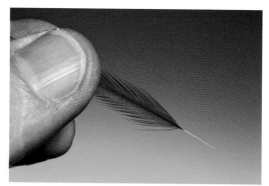

7 The dubbed body should be slender and even, but have a slight increasing taper towards the head, as shown. Finish with your tying thread approximately 3mm behind the hook eye.

8 Select a brown cock hackle and prepare this by stripping off the hackle fibers on each side of the stem as shown.

9 Secure the hackle with an X-tie so the hackle stands 90 degrees to the hook shank

10 Now tie down the hackle stem and trim away the surplus stem below the hook.

11 Attach a hackle plier to the hackle tip and carefully wrap your hackle in open, even turns backwards (and in a clockwise direction) towards the rear of the fly.

12 Once you have reached the rear of the body make a single turn of copper wire to catch in the hackle and hold it in place. Once secured, remove the hackle plier from the hackle, attach the plier to the wire, and wrap the wire rib (clockwise) in five or six even turns, forward over the hackle.

13 Secure the wire with a few turns of tying thread and snip off the surplus hackle tip at the rear of the hook.

14 While keeping tension on your tying thread, snap off the surplus wire rib. Make a few turns of tying thread over the wire end.

15 Now you will need some bleached elk hair. Hair that is straight and a little stiff is best suited for wings.

16 Cut a small bunch of the elk hair and with a fine comb or toothbrush remove all the underfur (this is the soft curly hair) and any short hairs from the cut base of the bunch.

17 Once the hair bunch is clean and free from underfur, place it (tips first) in a hair stacker to even up the tips.

18 Now spin your tying thread counterclockwise to give it a flat profile. (A round thread could cut the hair, when tightened). Hold the bunch in your left hand, place the tips level with the rear of the hook and make two loose turns of tying thread around the bunch and tighten, slowly, gently applying more pressure. But take care not to break your tying thread.

continued next page

19 Once secure make a few more tight turns of tying thread through the hair as you wrap forward.

20 You can now lift the bunch of hair (here to the right of the eye) and make a couple of whip finishes behind the hook eye. Now snip off your tying thread.

21 Holding the whole bunch of hair over the hook eye make a single neat cut to form the head, as shown. You can then apply a little drop of varnish to the finished whippings.

22 The finished Elk Hair Caddis.

How to Tie the
Copper Nymph

Two of the best-selling fly patterns in the world are the Copper John and the Brassie. Then came the Copper Nymph, in so many variants that it would take a whole book to cover them. What all three patterns have in common is a copper wire abdomen. This is my take on the Copper Nymph.

The copper wire abdomen adds extra weight to the pattern. It also adds some extra bling, and when it comes to river trout, they just love bling!

For this pattern I have taken the best materials for trout flies: pheasant tail, wood duck and peacock herl, along with the relatively new flat copper wire. All wrapped up in the style of a generic mayfly nymph which can be fished any way and any where.

When designing a fly, I always try to push all the trout's buttons. I study the most prominent features of the natural, i.e., tails, legs, head—and exaggerate them. I believe that this way, when the fly is drifting swiftly towards a feeding trout in pocket water, it's easily recognizable as food, and if you add a little extra bling as well, this may also attract the trout's attention.

If you don't have wood duck for the tail, you can also use mallard flank, or any other speckled hackle for that matter.

All flytyers accumulate more and more material as different patterns are tied over the years. You will, with time, come to understand which materials can be used for what, and what are their best substitutes.

The collecting and understanding of the materials we work with are all part of the pleasure of the craft, and something that you can look forward to...

WHAT YOU'LL LEARN

- Copper wire wrapped abdomen

- Overbody of pheasant tail

- Reverse pheasant tail legs

TYING TIPS

- Wrap your copper wire hand-over-hand so you don't twist it

- Choose a pheasant tail feather with long fibers

- Let the head varnish dry a little in-between coats

- You can use a round, heavy-gauge copper wire if you don't have flat

WATCH THE VIDEO

youtu.be/xMNcfZmSDfQ

Flytying for Beginners Copper Nymph with Barry Ord Clarke

Background technique videos 1–4, 8, 9 (pages 26–29)

THE DRESSING

Hook: Long shank nymph size 8–12
Thread: Black
Tail: Wood duck or mallard flank
Rib: UTC Ultra Wire (black)
Abdomen: Flat or round copper wire & pheasant tail
Thorax: Peacock herl
Wing case: Pheasant tail fibers
Legs: Pheasant tail
Head: Black thread

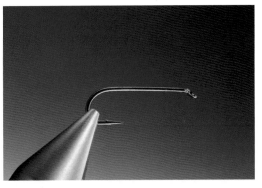

1 Secure your hook in the vise with the hook shank horizontal.

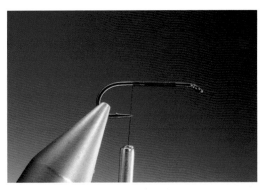

2 Attach your tying thread a little behind the hook eye and run a foundation back until your thread lies in line with the hook point.

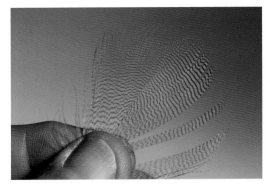

3 Now select a nicely marked wood duck or mallard flank feather which we are going to use for the tail.

4 Strip off a small bunch of fibers from the flank feather, taking care that the tips are aligned. The tail should be about two-thirds of the hook shank length. Tie this in on top of the hook shank as shown.

5 Cut about 20cm of black UTC Ultra wire. This is a super shiny varnished wire that works perfectly if you want extra bling.

6 Tie in the wire at the tail base as shown and using your tying thread, build up a slight taper on the abdomen.

continued next page

7 You will now need a length of about 25cm of medium flat or round copper wire for the abdomen.

8 Tie in the copper wire at the tail base and run your tying thread up the hook shank and into the thorax.

9 Cut a small bunch of cock pheasant tail fibers and tie these in by their tips at the tail base, on top of the hook shank. Take care that the underbody of tying thread is nice and even, this will give a better result when the wire is wrapped.

10 Take your flat copper wire and start to wrap it, hand over hand, so as not to twist it, in tight touching turns over the abdomen. If you have a rotary vise, you can use that to wrap your wire.

11 Continue over the body in touching turns until you have covered the whole abdomen with copper wire as shown. Tie off with a few turns of tying thread and snip off the excess copper wire.

12 Now straighten the pheasant tail fibers so that they are parallel and hold them in position with a couple of turns of tying thread at the thorax.

13 Take the black wire and make 5–6 evenly spaced open turns over the pheasant tail, to form the rib. Take care to keep the pheasant tail lying flat on top of the hook shank.

14 Now unwind the couple of turns of tying thread you made in Step 12, and fold back the pheasant tail. The wire rib will hold the pheasant tail in position. Tie off the black wire rib and snip off the excess wire.

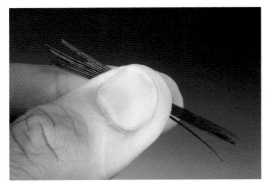

15 Now take another small bunch of pheasant tail fibers, about 10 or 12, and even the tips out.

16 Measure the tips of the pheasant tail out over the hook eye, so that when they are folded back they are long enough for the nymph legs, and tie down as shown.

17 This is how the thorax should look now from above. Don't cut off any of the pheasant tail fibers because these will be the wing case later.

18 Select a nice long fiber peacock herl.

continued next page

19 Cut a couple of centimeters off the point of the herl and tie in, with the tip end tight into the abdomen.

20 Attach a hackle plier to the herl and in close touching turns, wrap this forward over the thorax and secure a little behind the hook eye.

21 You can now fold the pheasant tail legs back, about half and half on each side and secure with a few wraps of tying thread.

22 Taking care to keep all the pheasant tail fibers straight and parallel, fold them over and tie down close to the thorax a little back from the hook eye.

23 Taking care, trim off the surplus pheasant tail over the hook eye at a slight angle. Now starting with your tying thread against the hook eye, wrap your way backwards over the cut ends to form a neat head.

24 Whip finish, remove your tying thread and varnish a neat black head. You may need to do a couple of coats of varnish. This is the underside view.

25 Copper Nymph viewed from above.

26 The finished Copper Nymph is perfect for searching fast-flowing pocket water.

continued next page

How to Tie the
Hair Wing Dun

Rather than show you a specific pattern for an adult mayfly, I believe it is more useful for you to learn the technique for tying a standard mayfly attractor. Once learned, you can adapt this pattern by changing the hook size, body and hackle color, along with the tail and wing material if desired, to match your own hatch. When fished on the water, this template represents the basic silhouette or footprint of an adult mayfly: tail, body, legs, and wings. The Hair Wing Dun is easy for a trout to recognize as food when it drifts overhead.

When selecting deer hair for the tail and wings, look for hair that has nice barred speckled tip markings. I believe, like hare's ear, this produces a very natural look to the fly.

Pay close attention to the proportions when cutting the bunches for the tail and wings, not only considering the size of each bunch required but also the tail and wing length in proportion to the hook size being used.

As a rule of thumb, the standard proportions for a dry fly are as follows:

Tail length = 2-2.5 x hook gape
Wing length = 2 x hook gape
Hackle length = 1.5 x hook gape

When tying in the wings, a common problem is ending up with a fat or bulky body. A sure way to avoid this is by cutting the surplus deer hair to a fine taper along the hook shank (Step 9). Once covered with a few wraps of tying thread, this will create a nice taper on the body and the bulk of the material will be under the wound hackle.

A deer hair tail requires a special technique to stop the deer hair from flaring and fanning out more than just a few degrees. Once you have cleaned and stacked a small bunch of deer hair for the tail, holding it in your left hand, measure the correct tail length and secure it mid-hook with a few tight wraps of tying thread, keeping hold of the tail all the time!

Once it's secure, spin your tying thread anti-clockwise so it gets a flat profile, then (Step 16) wrap your tying thread towards the tail as you slide your fingers holding the bunch of fibers backwards.

As you approach the tail base, slacken off the tying thread pressure with each wrap, not so that it's loose, but so it's just firm enough to hold the tail bunched in position, without flaring the hair. Then wrap your tying thread back up the hook shank, making each turn a little tighter as you approach the centre of the body.

WHAT YOU'LL LEARN

- The importance of selecting good deer hair and cleaning it well

- How to split and hold in place the hair wings

- Traditional collar hackle

TYING TIPS

- Spend time cleaning and preparing your deer hair for best results

- Less is more. Carefully measure the amount of hair for the tail and wing

WATCH THE VIDEO

youtu.be/HJpcM0CvxMw

Flytying for Beginners
Hair Wing Dun with
Barry Ord Clarke

THE DRESSING

Hook: Standard dry fly hook size 10–16
Thread: Gray
Body: Super Fine dubbing grey or blue dun
Wings: Fine natural deer hair, long hair is easier to work with
Hackle: Grizzle dyed brown

Background technique videos 1–9 (pages 26–29)

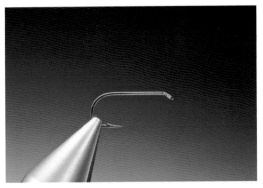

1 Secure your dry fly hook in the vise with the hook shank horizontal.

2 Load your bobbin with grey tying thread.

3 Attach your tying thread to the hook shank and make a short foundation as shown.

4 Select some natural deer hair.

5 Cut a small bunch, enough for both the wings. Now clean the hair, making sure that you remove all the soft underfur and the shorter hairs.

6 Check that the amount is correct for two wings when split. Now even up the hair tips in a hair stacker.

continued next page

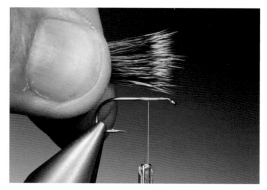

7 Carefully remove the hair from the stacker. Holding it in your left hand, measure the wing length against the hook.

8 While holding the hair in position with your left hand, secure with a few tight turns of tying thread. Keeping hold of the hair make a few more wraps of tying thread rearward. Don't let go of the hair with your left hand!

9 Lift the hair bunch with your left hand and trim off the excess at a slight angle as shown.

10 Spin your tying thread anti-clockwise so it gets a flat profile and cover the whole base of the deer hair wing to form a smooth taper.

11 Lift the wing vertically and place a few wraps of tying thread tight in front of of the wing. This will keep the wing upright at 90°.

12 Using your dubbing needle you can now divide the wing into two even amounts.

13 Once the wings are divided, secure them with a figure-of-eight tie. This will keep the wings apart.

14 Now, to keep the deer hair in each wing together in a tight bunch, make a few wraps around the base of each wing. Finish with your tying thread mid-body.

15 Cut, clean, and stack a smaller bunch of deer hair for the tail.

16 Tie in the tail hair as described on page 114.

17 Once the tail is secure wrap your tying thread forward again towards the wing base.

18 Carefully trim away the excess deer hair and make a few wraps of tying thread over the ends.

continued next page

19 You will now need some blue dun or grey Super Fine dubbing.

20 Wind your tying thread back to the tail base. Now spin a little dubbing onto your tying thread and wrap it along the hook shank towards the wing, tightening the dubbing as you go. This will create a slender body for your dry fly.

21 Cover the whole body with dubbing as shown. Finish with your tying thread just behind the wing base.

22 Prepare a hackle by stripping off the fibers each side of the base of the stem.

23

Tie in your hackle by the stem with a X-tie (see Glossary page 6), so the hackle stands approximately 90° from the hook shank.

24 Now carefully wrap your hackle forward, each turn close into the previous. When you reach the rear of the wings, make the next turn in front of the wings and continue forward to just behind the hook eye. Secure the hackle and trim off the excess.

25 Make a couple of whip finishes and give the head a drop or two of varnish.

26 The finished Hair Wing Dun, seen from above.

continued next page

Further Tips for the Beginner

STORING YOUR MATERIALS

No matter how small or large your tying kit is, try to give your materials a storage system that is easy to access. This dramatically reduces the time you lose searching for materials you need, which increases tying time, efficiency, and enjoyment.

I also recommend you purchasing one large and a few small, airtight, clear plastic boxes for storing your materials. These boxes will keep your natural materials—feathers, hair, and fur—safe from moth and beetle larvae. Clear plastic boxes let you see what materials or tools are stored in them, without having to open them all to find what you are looking for.

If you do find that your materials have become infected with any of these vermin, place ALL your natural materials in a plastic box or bag and put it in deep freezer for four or five days. This should exterminate any unwanted guests!

PROPORTIONS

Tying proportions will always be debated among flytyers as to what is life-like, or best for catching fish, or aesthetically pleasing to the tyer.

Try to settle on your favorite proportions for each pattern. This will enable you to prep your materials more accurately, and after much practice will make each fly identical to the last.

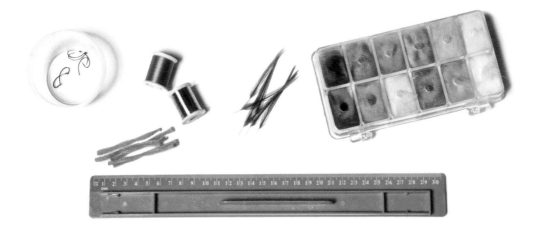

Always have a 30cm ruler on your tying bench, easily accessible between you and the vise. In this position you can quickly measure materials to the correct length, when both tying and prepping. This will not only improve your fly proportions, getting wing, hackle, and other materials a uniform length, but it will also save you wasting materials if you cut the correct length needed of tinsel or floss from a spool.

PREP YOUR MATERIALS BEFORE TYING

When you intend to tie a half dozen or more of the same pattern, prepare all the hooks and materials needed, for the correct amount to be tied. First count the correct number of hooks needed. Then place them in a small plastic container, then prep the other materials. Select all the hackles in the correct size and prepare these by stripping off the downy section and trimming the stem. If you are using hair, cut all the bunches needed and clean and stack them. These can then be placed in a simple hair holder ready for use. If you are using tinsel or floss, cut them to the correct length, and so on... When all the materials are ready, clear an area on your tying bench and lay the hooks and materials out in the correct order to be used.

TIDY WORKSPACE

Keeping your tying area tidy and your tools and materials organized will help you locate the necessary materials and tools at a glance and within arm's reach. Being halfway through a procedure and not being able to find the tool or material you need to complete it, is very frustrating.

LIGHTING

The lighting on your tying area is as important as any of your tools. Tying under poor lighting will prove difficult, especially if you're tying small flies, but it will also be tiring for your eyes. I recommend using a good bright light, preferably on a flexible arm for easy positioning. The use of a daylight-corrected bulb in your lamp will also help you tie better and for longer.

Index

Index

The Author

Born in England, Barry Ord Clarke is an internationally acclaimed flytyer, photographer, and author. He has won medals in the world's most prestigious flytying competitions, and his own flies can be seen in the iconic Flyfishers' Club collection in London and in the Catskill Master Fly Collection in the Catskill Museum in the United States.

In 2016, he was awarded the coveted Claudio D'Angelo award for Best International Fly Tyer. In 2018, he completed seven years' work with Marc Petitjean for the book *Petitjean CDC*.

For the past twenty-seven years he has lived in Norway where he works as a professional photographer and flytying consultant for Mustad and Veniard Ltd.

You can find Barry's flytying demonstrations on his blog and YouTube channel, The Feather Bender.

Below: Barry's flytying den in Norway. Warning: your burgeoning hobby could lead to this...

© David Edwards

THE FEATHER BENDER
EST. 1961

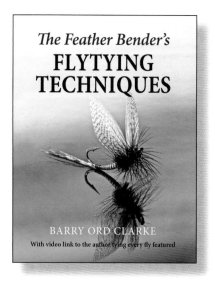

What the critics say about the author's previous book

The Feather Bender's FLYTYING TECHNIQUES

"I can't recall another project like this crossing my desk. Highly recommended."
– Flyfishing & Flytying magazine

"For those who follow thefeatherbender.com, Barry's regular blog and flytying videos on YouTube, this book is an essential addition. For those who don't know Barry's work, this would be a great introduction to someone who I consider to be amongst the world's best modern flytyers." **– Flydresser magazine**

"Barry is the consummate flytyer, possibly the best that I have been fortunate to have encountered over my years of tying. His style of flytying is unique, and he produces what is close to, in my opinion, the perfect fly. Bound to be a true modern classic."
– Freshwater Fishing, Australia

"When a great photographer, fly tyer and instructor writes a book, it's likely to become a great book." **– Global Flyfisher**

"Barry's most innovative book to date. I struggle to label this book as one for beginners or one for experts: I see it as a book for every flytyer, at every level."
– Fly Line magazine, Italy

"The whole thing is genius! First to be able to watch Barry tie the fly and then later, in your own time, to go through the 'step-by-step guide' while you tie. This book is for everyone who ties flies – from beginners to full-blown professionals.

"Looking through this over 250-page book and thinking about the 28 videos which have been made for each of the patterns, one can only wonder about the reasonable price! I can't call it anything less than a masterpiece. Whoever buys this book will get more than their money's worth!" **– Flugfiske i Norden, Sweden**

"A ground-breaking fly tying book."' **– Trout Fisher magazine, NZ**

"In addition to the beautiful photographs, Barry has enlisted modern technology. Use your mobile phone to scan the QR code on the relevant page and up will pop a video showing Barry tying the very pattern." **– Orvis, USA**

The Feather Bender beginners' flies on YouTube

To watch the YouTube videos of the basic flytying techniques and of the author tying each of the flies, you can follow any of these options:

1. To use the QR code: open the camera on your smartphone or chosen device. Hold the camera over the red QR code and your web browser will pop up automatically, leading you to the YouTube video of Barry tying that very fly.

2. Or key in to your browser the URL (YouTube link) as shown in the book immediately beneath the "Watch the Video" heading.

3. Or type in to your web browser the full fly title as it appears at the start of each step-by-step tying section of the book. The video will come up.

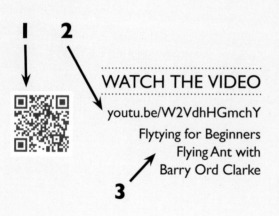

WATCH THE VIDEO

youtu.be/W2VdhHGmchY

Flytying for Beginners
Flying Ant with
Barry Ord Clarke